A DICTIONARY
OF
TERMS USED IN MEASUREMENTS
AND GUIDANCE

By

EARL BENNETT SOUTH

Assistant Professor of Education
In Charge of Tests and Measurements
New York State College for Teachers
Albany, New York

FIRST EDITION

THE PSYCHOLOGICAL CORPORATION
522 FIFTH AVENUE
New York City
1938

COPYRIGHT, 1939
EARL BENNETT SOUTH

PREFACE

The purpose of this glossary is to make accessible to the student dealing with the problem of testing, the definitions of the terms of the field. There has been no attempt to make the list of terms exhaustive, but rather to include the terms which are most commonly used by writers in the field of mental testing, educational testing, statistics, and guidance. In this list there are many terms which are synonymous. Those which are most commonly used or are preferred by writers are defined. In many instances it has been impossible to improve upon the statements of other writers, and in such instances exact quotations have been used. This is especially true in definitions of terms which are common to all persons using them.

The author has employed the abbreviations which are most frequently used. Two or more references are usually given in order that these may be consulted by the reader who wishes a more detailed discussion or illustrations. These references are limited to seventeen well-known texts covering the various fields.

The following is a complete list of the sources mentioned:

BRUECKNER, L. J., AND MELBY, E. O. *Diagnostic and Remedial Teaching.* Houghton-Mifflin and Co., 1931. 598 pp.

FREEMAN, F. N. *Mental Tests.* Houghton-Mifflin and Co., 1926. 503 pp.

GREENE, H. A., AND JORGENSEN, A. N. *Use and Interpretation of Elementary School Tests.* Longmans Green and Co., 1935. 530 pp.

GREENE, H. A., AND JORGENSEN, A. N. *Use and Interpretation of High School Tests.* Longmans Green and Co., 1936. 614 pp.

JONES, A. J. *Principles of Guidance* (Second Edition) McGraw Hill & Co., 1934. 456 pp.

KELLEY, T. L. *Interpretation of Educational Measurements.* World Book Co., 1927. 363 pp.

McCALL, W. A. *How to Measure in Education.* Macmillan and Co., 1922. 416 pp.

MONROE, W. S. *Introduction to the Theory of Educational Measurements.* Houghton-Mifflin and Co., 1923. 364 pp.

MONROE, W. S., DE VOSS, J. C., AND KELLY, F. J. *Educational Tests and Measurements.* Houghton-Mifflin and Co., 1924. 521 pp.

ODELL, C. W. *Educational Measurement in the High School.* D. Appleton-Century Co., 1930. 641 pp.

ODELL, C. W. *Statistical Method in Education.* D. Appleton-Century Co., 1935. 457 pp.

ORLEANS, J. S. *Measurements in Education.* Thomas Nelson and Sons, 1937. 461 pp.

OTIS, A. S. *Statistical Method in Educational Measurements.* World Book Co., 1925. 337 pp.

PINTNER, R. *Intelligence Testing.* Henry Holt and Co., 1931. 555 pp.

PRESSEY, S. L., AND COLE, L. *Introduction to the Use of Standard Tests.* World Book Co., 1926. 263 pp.

RUCH, G. M., AND STODDARD, G. D. *Tests and Measurements in High School Instruction.* World Book Co., 1927. 381 pp.

SYMONDS, P. *Measurement in Secondary Education.* Macmillan and Co., 1927. 588 pp.

I wish to express my thanks to the authors and publishers of these books, who, by granting permission to use materials, have made this glossary possible. I wish to express my appreciation to Dr. C. W. Odell who gave me special permission to use quotations from the University of Illinois Bulletin No. 28, published in 1928 and entitled, "A Glossary of Three Hundred Terms Used in Educational Measurement and Research," and to D. Appleton-Century Co. for their permission to quote liberally from the two earlier Odell volumes. I am indebted to Dr. J. Allan Hicks, Professor of Guidance, New York State College for Teachers, Albany, New York, who read the manuscript and suggested certain terms closely related to guidance. Finally I am indebted to Dr. George K. Bennett, Director of the Test Division of the Psychological Corporation, as well as to the Corporation for the sponsoring of this project.

EARL BENNETT SOUTH.

Albany, New York,
November 1, 1938.

A

A. A. Abbreviation for achievement age, also accomplishment age, and attainment age.

A. D. Abbreviation for average deviation, better called mean deviation.

A. M. Sometimes used as the abbreviation for assumed mean.

A. Q. Abbreviation for achievement quotient, also accomplishment quotient and attainment quotient.

A. R. Abbreviation for achievement ratio, also accomplishment ratio, and attainment ratio.

Ability. Actual power to perform an act. It may be inherited or acquired. The term capacity, often used to denote the same thing, usually means undeveloped power and therefore is largely innate.

Ability Grouping. Practice of sub-subdividing a group of pupils into smaller groups of relatively equal ability, either in some one subject or in general ability; also called *Homogeneous Grouping and Sectioning According to Ability*.

Abscissa. The horizontal axis in reference to a two-dimensional chart.

Abstract Intelligence. The effective use of abstract concepts and symbols in dealing with new situations. Such tests test the ability to respond to symbols of various sorts, such as words, numbers, letters, and the like. At its highest levels abstract intelligence is seen in the reactions of the student and philosopher dealing with the relations of things symbolized in words or numbers or mathematical formulae.
    Pintner, R., Intelligence Testing, p. 55.

Accidental Error. Synonymous with variable error.

Accomplishment Age (A. A.). Sometimes used as synonymous with achievement age.

Accomplishment Quotient (A. Q.). Sometimes used as synonymous with achievement quotient.

Accomplishment Ratio (A. R.). A rarely employed term, synonymous with achievement ratio.

Accuracy. Accuracy refers in a general way to freedom from error. The term has two more or less special or technical uses in the field of educational measurement. In one of these it refers to a characteristic or dimension of pupil achievement and in this sense is very nearly synonymous with quality. It is, however, slightly more restricted in its meaning than quality and may be defined as the correctness or freedom from error of pupils' responses. In its second sense it is employed in connection with the freedom from error of test scores and other measures. In this connection it is sometimes used as synonymous with reliability, but really has a broader meaning since reliability is concerned only with variable errors whereas accuracy depends upon freedom from both constant and variable errors. *See constant, quality, reliable, variable error.*

> Monroe, W. S., Introduction to the Theory of Educational Measurement, p. 180f.
> Symonds, P., Measurement in Secondary Education, pp. 123, 288f.

Achievement Age (A. A.). The age equivalent of a pupil's score on an achievement test is usually referred to as his achievement age. A given achievement age, such as 10 years and 8 months or, as it is occasionally expressed, 128 months, means that the pupil who earns this score has done as well on the given test as the average or medium pupil whose chronological age is 10 years and 8 months. In actual practice an achievement age is generally established by determining the average or median achievement of a group of pupils whose mental age is the desired amount, in this case 10 years and 8 months. *See age norm, age score.*

> Monroe, W. S., Introduction to the Theory of Educational Measurement, p. 155f.

Achievement Quotient (A. Q.). This term is applied to a kind of score which shows the relationship between a pupil's actual achievement and what he should achieve according to his mental capacity. The measure of what he should achieve commonly used is the average or median achieved by pupils of his chronological or mental age. Since, as was explained under achievement age, the average achievement score of a group of pupils of a given mental or chronological age is called an achievement age of the same amount, a pupil's achievement quotient might be secured by dividing his achievement age by either his mental age or his chronological age. The former—that is, division by the mental age—was first suggested and is the common practice, so that usually

$$A.\,Q. = \frac{A.\,A.}{M.\,A.}.$$

Unfortunately, however, a few persons have introduced confusion by dividing by the chronological age instead of the mental age, so that sometimes

$$A.\,Q. = \frac{A.\,A.}{C.\,A.}.$$

Since it is the purpose of the achievement quotient to compare a pupil's actual achievement with what he should achieve, it seems distinctly preferable to use his mental age, which is a measure of his ability, as a denominator rather than his chronological age, which merely measures the length of time he has happened to live. *See quotient score.*

    Freeman, F. N., Mental Tests, p. 285f.
    Kelley, T. L., Interpretation of Educational Measurements, pp. 6f., 22f.
    Monroe, W. S., Introduction to the Theory of Educational Measurement, p. 157f.

Achievement Ratio (A. R.). Because the achievement quotient is computed in two ways and hence has two different meanings, it has been proposed that the situation be simplified by restricting it to one meaning and applying the term achievement ratio to the other. Unfortunately there has been no general agreement as to which expression should be called the achievement ratio. It appears, however, that the most frequent use of achievement ratio has been to refer to the result obtained by dividing achievement age by mental age; that is,

$$A.\,R. = \frac{A.\,A.}{M.\,A.}.$$

Its use in this sense is urged by those who secure the achievement quotient by dividing achievement age by chronological age. *See ratio score.*

    Kelley, T. L., Interpretation of Educational Measurements, p. 8.

>   Monroe, W. S., DeVoss, J. C., and Kelly, F. J., Educational Tests and Measurements, p. 381.
>   Otis, A. S., Statistical Method in Educational Measurements, p. 172f.

Achievement Test. This name is applied to a test which measures a pupil's knowledge or mastery of the subject matter taught in school. In other words, such a test measures what the pupil has actually learned rather than his capacity to learn.

Adjustment. Adapting one's self to new situations, to new modes of behavior. There are various types of adjustments such as social, vocational, and educational.

>   Jones, A. J., Principles of Guidance, pp. 49, 289, 297, 302–306, 389, 397.

Advisor. *See counselor.*

Age, Basal. A term used in connection with the Stanford-Binet Intelligence Test. The highest age level at which all of the tests for that age-level are passed.

Age Calibration. A process of standardization of a test in regard to age levels; most often the chronological is used.

Age-Grade-Table. A table showing the number of children of each age in each school grade. Often those who are above grade level and those below grade level are also indicated.

Age, Mental. *See mental age.*

Age Norm. An age norm expresses the average or median achievement, intelligence, or other characteristic of a group of pupils of the designated chronological age. In determining age norms for achievement tests, the pupils are frequently grouped according to mental age as this type of grouping is easier to secure than one based on chronological age. Since a given mental age represents the average intelligence of pupils of the same chronological age, the result is the same as if chronological age groups were used. Unless otherwise stated, an age norm is usually the average or median of scores made by pupils ranging from the designated age up to the next. For example, a score given as the norm for nine-year-old children is ordinarily understood to be for children who are at least nine years of age but not yet ten. *See norm.*

>   Ruch, G. M., and Stoddard, G. B., Tests and Measurement in High School Instruction, p. 346f.
>   Symonds, P., Measurement in Secondary Education, p. 255f.

Age Scale. A series of tests in which the units of measurement are the differences between successive age norms. Each difference is treated as if equal to all others.

Age Score. Pupils' scores, both on tests of intelligence and on those of achievement, are frequently expressed in terms of ages, the mental age being used in the case of intelligence and the achievement age in that of achievement. Point scores are transmuted into age scores on the basis of age norms. For example, if a pupil makes a score of 48 upon a particular test and 48 is the age norm for nine years, this pupil is said to have an age score of nine years. An age score of any given amount indicates that the pupil earning it is just at the average of pupils of this age. *See achievement age, age norm, educational age, mental age, social age, subject age.*

Freeman, F. N., Mental Tests, p. 81f.
Monroe, W. S., DeVoss, J. C., and Kelly, F. J., Educational Tests and Measurements, p. 380.

Age Variability Unit. Among the units employed in educational and psychological measurement is the age variability unit. Such a unit is a function of the variability of a single age group. It is assumed that the variability of a group of pupils of any single age may be equated to that of a group of any other age. Therefore some function of this variability, such as the difference between the average score made by the pupils of an age group and the score dividing the upper 25 per cent from the lower 75 per cent of the same group, is used as a standard unit and considered equal to the same function for a group of any other age.

McCall, W. A., How to Measure in Education, p. 272f.

Alertness Test. A proposed substitute for intelligence test. The use of such a term implies that one's quickness in the several mental functions is due to a single cause, trait, or faculty. Spearman's hypothesis of g may be an illustration. The above term is also an attempt to avoid the use of the term intelligence.

Pintner, R., Intelligence Testing, Ch. 4.

Alienation Coefficient. A term applied to the expression $(1 - r^2)^{\frac{1}{2}}$ (wherein r is a product moment correlation) which measures the lack of relation between two correlated variables or traits.

Odell, C. W., Statistical Method in Education, p. 594.

Alpha Tests. A set of mental tests first used in the United States Army in 1917–1918 at the time of the World War. These tests consisted of eight different types of tests: directions, arithmetical problems, practical judgment, synonyms-antonyms, disarranged sentences, number series completion, analogies, and information. These tests were used for group testing.

Alternative Test. This expression is often applied to one of the chief types of tests included by the new examination and used in many standardized tests. Each item in this type of test permits the pupil a choice between two possibilities, one of which is right and the other wrong. The most common varieties of exercises of this sort are true-false statements and yes-no questions, but others are sometimes used. *See true-false test, yes-no test.*

    Greene, H. A., and Jorgensen, A. N., Use and Interpretation of High School Tests, Ch. 4.
    Odell, C. W., Objective Measurement in the High School, p. 9f.

Analogies Test. Such a test is of the form of the ordinary mathematical proportion, with one of the four terms or occasionally even two of them omitted. An example from the field of algebra is: a^2 is to a^6 as x^3 is to ——; another, from grammar: ran is to run as —— is to sit. This type of exercise is often used in general intelligence tests and sometimes in achievement tests.

    Odell, C. W., Objective Measurement, p. 27.
    Pitner, R., Intelligence Testing, Ch. 7.

Analogy Test. Occasionally used as synonymous with miniature test.

Aptitude. A natural or acquired disposition or capacity for a particular purpose, knowledge, or skill such as ability in a language, mechanical aptitude, etc.

Aptitude Test. Synonymous with prognostic test.

Arithmetic Average (Aver. or A.). This is the same as the ordinary average, better called the mean.

Arithmetic Mean (M.). Synonymous with mean.

Array. A single row or column of a correlation table including the frequencies which fall in it is called an array. In other words, an array includes all of the measures in a correlation table which fall within a single class or interval of one of the two variables concerned. For example, if age divided into intervals of years is correlated with height by inches, all of the frequencies for each age class, such as 10 years, form an array, as likewise do all for each height class, such as 52 inches. *See correlation table.*

Association Test. There is some difference of practice as to the use of this expression. It has been applied to several kinds of tests often included in standardized and new-type tests. Probably its most frequent use has been to designate tests in each exercise of which one, or sometimes more, terms are given to which the pupils are asked to add others closely associated. Sometimes the association is described as *fixed* to designate the fact that the pupil is expected to recognize certain requirements in responding to the exercise; in other cases it is *free*. Thus a list of words may be given for each of which the pupils are to supply a synonym or perhaps an antonym, a list of cities may be given for each of which an important product is to be named, or a list of historical characters for each of whom one important event is to be given.

Assumed Mean (Ass. M. or A. M.). In the short method of computing the mean, the standard and mean deviations, and various other statistical expressions, use is made of an assumed or guessed mean. In other words, the person making the calculations inspects the distribution of data and estimates or assumes the value of the mean. This assumed mean is always taken as being the mid-point of a class or interval, and it is almost always desirable that the mid-point selected be as near as possible to the true mean; that is, nearer to it than the mid-point of any other class would be to that mean. If, however, the guess made is not accurate enough to produce this result, no error will be introduced into any of the succeeding calculations except in the case of the mean deviation.

Odell, C. W., Statistical Method in Education, p. 69.
Otis, A. S., Statistical Method in Educational Measurements, p. 191.

Assumption. A great deal, if not all, of educational research, especially in the field of measurements, is either explicitly or implicitly based upon assumptions. In some cases these assumptions are apparent facts or principles which cannot be definitely proven, but which appear to be in accord with such evidence as is available. In other cases the assumptions made are rather of the nature of limitations or perhaps bases for investigation; that is, one may assume that certain things are facts and proceed to investigate or determine what results or conclusions follow. It is probably true that many more assumptions are made implicitly than are definitely stated. In many studies it is, for example, assumed without proof or even without comment that children should attend school, that they should study certain subjects, that they should progress from grade to grade, and so forth.

> Monroe, W. S., Introduction to the Theory of Educational Measurement, p. 21f.

Attainment Age (A. A.). Sometimes used as synonymous with achievement age.

Attainment Quotient (A. Q.). Sometimes used as synonymous with achievement quotient.

Attainment Ratio (A. R.). Sometimes used as synonymous with achievement ratio.

Attenuation. If, as is practically always the case, there are chance or variable errors in the measures or scores of either one or both of two variables involved in a correlation, the effect of these errors is to lower the obtained value of the coefficient of correlation below what it would be if the measures or scores were accurate. This effect—that is, the lowering of the value of the coefficient—is called attentuation. If two series of measures of each of the variables are available, any one of several formulae may be employed to correct for attenuation and give approximately true value of the coefficient of correlation.

> Odell, C. W., Statistical Method in Education, p. 215f.

Aussage Test. A test of the fidelity with which certain past experiences are reported. Results depend on perception and observation as well as memory.

Average (Aver. or A.). The term average is employed in two different senses, but to avoid confusion it is better to limit it to one. This is its use as a general term to include the mean, median, mode, geometric mean, and all other measures of central tendency. Its other use is that common in elementary arithmetic and in ordinary conversation. In this sense it refers to the sum of a number of measures or quantities divided by their number. It is recommended by most statisticians, however, that the term mean be used in this latter sense. *See central tendency, mean.*

> Odell, C. W., Statistical Method in Education, p. 66.
> Otis, A. S., Statistical Method in Educational Measurements, p. 6f.

Average Deviation (A. D.). Synonymous with mean deviation.

Average Error. The average amount by which the separate values of a series of measurements differ from the standard.

Average Score. The arithmetical mean score.

Averages, Law of. The statement that the average of a group of observations has a greater probability of occurrence than has any single observation.

B

b. Abbreviation for the coefficient of regression (beta). Subscripts, usually x and y or 1 and 2 are employed to distinguish between the regression coefficients of the two variables concerned in an ordinary regression or correlation.

Ball-and-Field Test. A test of practical intelligence in which the testee is asked how he would go about searching for a ball lost in a field of a circular shape. This test was included in the 1916 Terman revision of the Stanford-Binet.

Basal Age. *See base year.*

Base Year. When a subject passes perfectly all the tests assigned to a given year (in a Stanford-Binet or analogous age-grade test) and passes or is assumed to pass all tests below this point in the scale, this highest year is taken as the base year and to that base, credits are added for passing additional tests above the base in determining his mental age.

Battery of Tests. A group of several tests, usually achievement tests in several subjects, given pupils as part of a single testing program either at one time or within a short period of time, is frequently called a battery of tests. The term is more or less but not absolutely synonymous with the expression general survey test.

Orleans, J. S., Measurement in Education, p. 106.

Best-Answer Test. Synonymous with multiple-answer test.

Best-Reason Test. This is a variety of the best-answer or multiple-answer test. The suggested answers are reasons rather than mere facts or other items.

Beta Tests. A series of mental tests first used in the United States Army in 1917–1918. They are designed primarily for illiterates and persons deficient in English, the instructions being given in sign language. These tests are companion tests to the Alpha tests used in the Army.

Bi-Modal. A graph or distribution which has two modes; that is, two points at which the frequencies or numbers of cases are greater than on either side of each, is called bi-modal. In such cases the mode at which the number of cases is the greater is called the major mode; the other, the minor mode.

Binet-Simon Scale. A series of graded tests designed by Alfred Binet and Th. Simon in 1905, in order to rate the intelligence of children. These tests were revised by Binet in 1908 and 1911, and later introduced into this country by Henry Goddard. There are several revisions in use. The Terman-Merrill of 1937 is the most recent and the most commonly used today.

B-Score. This expression is practically synonymous with grade score. It consists of one figure in units' place indicating the grade and one in tenths' place indicating the month of the school year, thus assuming a school year of ten months. To illustrate, a B-score of 4.3 is the average for fourth-grade pupils in the third month of the school year. Point scores are transmuted into B-scores by the same general method as into any derived scores; that is, the average or median point score for each given grade and each month of the school year is determined. The name B-score was proposed in honor of Binet and Buckingham.

Biserial r. The coefficient of correlation between two variables, one of which is continuous while the other has only two values. For example, biserial r might be used to express the relationship between age at graduation and sex.

Odell, C. W., Statistical Method in Education, p. 321.

Block-Design Test. A test of intelligence, involving the assembling of painted cubes so as to form a pattern or design; e.g., Koh's Block Design Test.

Brown-Spearman Formula. A formula for estimating the reliability of a test.

C

C. A. Abbreviation for chronological age.

C. B. Abbreviation for coefficient of brightness.

C. I. Abbreviation for the coefficient of intelligence.

Cancellation Test. A test of speed in the discrimination of forms. In these tests a single or a double letter is to be crossed out. The letter or letters are arranged in a random order.

Capacity. The full potentiality of an individual; his ability. *See ability.*

Case Method. A method of investigation recently used in education in which the data or facts are classified in groups, classes or histories which will tend to give a more complete picture of the situation and thus help in making analysis. It was used earlier in clinical and social work.

Jones, A. J., Principles of Guidance, pp. 198–203.

Cause and Effect Test. This name is applied to a form of test often used as part of a new-type examination, and also sometimes in standardized tests. Each exercise therein consists of several words or phrases one or more of which are causes and the remaining ones, effects. Pupils are instructed to mark all the causes or all the effects by underlining or by some other method. This form of test is sometimes classed under association tests and also sometimes under multiple-answer tests.

CAVD. Letters referring to the four kinds of content used in the I. E. R. Intelligence Scale, namely: Completion, Arithmetic, Vocabulary, and Directions. These tests were constructed by Thorndike of the Institute of Educational Research.

Pintner, R., Intelligence Testing, pp. 209–210.

Centile. A division obtained by arranging all the cases in order from low to high and dividing them into 100 groups or ranks with the lowest as the first centile, etc. Normally, each such centile has a different range of scores but the same number of cases; viz., $\frac{1}{100}$ of the total number. Groups analogous to the centile are made by dividing the total into three divisions—Tertiles; into four divisions—Quartiles; into five divisions—Quintiles; into ten divisions—Deciles, etc.

The term Percentile rank instead of centile rank is a misnomer: the pth percentile is not a rank or group of cases but the point below which just p percent of the cases occur. Thus we may have a zero percentile but no actually attained 100 percentile; centile ranks, in contrast, begin with 1, and include the 100th centile.

Central Tendency. The point on the scale about which the measures composing a frequency distribution tend to group themselves is called the central tendency. Any average, using this term in its wider sense, is a measure of central tendency. *See average, mean, median, mode.*

    Odell, C. W., Statistical Method in Education, p. 66.
    Otis, A. S., Statistical Method in Educational Measurements, p. 6f.

Class. In education, a group of individuals gathered together for more or less simultaneous instruction. In statistics, when the data are arranged in order of magnitude and arbitrarily divided into parts with an equal range of scores or number of units for each, that range is the Class Interval while the limits defining each such part or the cases falling within it define a class.

Class Interval (i). This expression, sometimes shortened to interval, refers to the width of a step, class, or group in which measures are grouped in a frequency table. For example, if in tabulating pupils' ages all those from six years up to but not including six years and six months are grouped together, those from six years and six months up to but not including seven years are also grouped together, and so on, the class interval is six months.

    Odell, C. W., Statistical Method in Education, pp. 19, 73, 80.
    Otis, A. S., Statistical Method in Educational Measurements, p. 37.

Classification Test. This expression is employed in at least two senses. One usage refers to any test designed primarily for classifying school pupils for purposes of instruction. The second meaning refers to a variety of the new examination. Each exercise in this variety consists of a number of terms several of which are alike in some way. The pupils may be instructed to underline or otherwise indicate the words which are alike or to mark those which are unlike the majority.

    Pintner, R., Intelligence Testing, p. 188.

Code Test. A type of mental test question in which the testee is required to translate as quickly as possible a series of code signs.

Coefficient of Brightness (C. B.). The coefficient of brightness is a rarely used measure of intelligence compared with the chronological age, similar to but not identical with the intelligence quotient. Theoretically the two are the same for children up to the age of fourteen years. In the extreme ranges, however, it is unlikely that they will correspond exactly. The coefficient of brightness is obtained by dividing a pupil's score by the score which is normal for his age. This measure has now been displaced by the index of brightness. *See index of brightness.*

Otis, A. S., Statistical Method in Educational Measurements, p. 153f.

Coefficient of Correlation (r). There are a number of numerical expressions or indices of correlation which may be called coefficients of correlation. The term is, however, generally restricted so that it applies only to the one obtained by the product-moment method and abbreviated by r, which is the most frequently used measure of correlation. This is sometimes called the Pearson coefficient because its use was strongly advocated by the English statistician, Karl Pearson. It is an index of rectilinear or straight-line correlation or relationship which ranges in value from $+1.00$ through zero to -1.00. A value of $+1.00$ indicates perfect positive correlation, one of zero no correlation at all, and -1.00 perfect negative correlation. The basic formula for it is

$$r = \frac{\sum xy}{N \sigma_x \sigma_y} \text{ or } \frac{\sum xy}{\sqrt{\sum x^2 \cdot \sum y^2}}.$$

See correlation, negative correlation, positive correlation.

Odell, C. W., Statistical Method in Education, p. 151.
Otis, A. S., Statistical Method in Educational Measurements, p. 181f.

Coefficient of Correspondence. The coefficient of correspondence may be defined as the per cent of individuals who have the same relative position within the whole group in one series of measures as they do in the other of the two being compared. It will be seen that the meaning of this definition depends upon the interpretation of the words "have the same relative position". Since different statisticians and others have defined "the same relative position" differently, there are a number of ways in which coefficients of correspondence have been computed.

Odell, C. W., Statistical Method in Education, p. 231.

Coefficient of Intelligence (C. I.). In connection with a few intelligence tests it has been recommended that instead of using the intelligence quotient, the ratio of a child's score to the average score of a child of his own age, called the coefficient of intelligence, be employed. As is true in the case of the intelligence quotient, a coefficient of intelligence above 1.00 indicates superior mentality, one of 1.00 exactly normal or average mentality, and one below 1.00 inferior mentality. Because of the difference in methods of computation it cannot be assumed that a coefficient of intelligence of any given amount other than 1.00 means exactly the same as an intelligence quotient of the same amount.

Freeman, F. N., Mental Tests, p. 134, 281f.

Coefficient of Multiple Correlation

$$(R_{1 \cdot 23 \cdots n} \text{ or } R_{1(23 \ldots n)})$$

The coefficient of multiple correlation is a product-moment coefficient derived from ordinary or simple product-moment coefficient of correlation. *See multiple correlation, product moment correlation.*

Odell, C. W., Statistical Method in Education, p. 283.
Otis, A. S., Statistical Method in Educational Measurements, p. 283.

Coefficient of Partial Correlation

$$(r_{12 \cdot 34 \cdots n}, r_{123 \cdot 45 \cdots n}, \text{etc.})$$

The coefficient of partial correlation is derived from simple product-moment coefficients of correlation and is itself a product-moment coefficient measuring the degree of partial correlation. *See partial correlation, product-moment correlation.*

Odell, C. W., Statistical Method in Education, p. 263.
Otis, A. S., Statistical Method in Educational Measurements, p. 232f.

Coefficient of Regression (b). This is an expression which shows the average change in one or two associated variables for each unit change in the other. Thus if the coefficient of regression of one variable on the other is .75 it means that on the average the first variable will increase .75 for every increase of one unit in the other, and will decrease .75 unit for every decrease of one. The formula for the coefficient of regression of one variable, X, on the other, Y is

$$b_x = r \frac{\sigma_x}{\sigma_y}$$

Odell, C. W., Statistical Method in Education, p. 240.

Coefficient of Reliability. The coefficient of reliability is merely the coefficient of correlation between the scores secured from two applications of the same test or of duplicate forms thereof. The two applications should be separated by only a short interval of time so that as little change as possible will occur in the intelligence and knowledge of the pupils tested. A coefficient of reliability above .90 is relatively high for a group test. Most of those of the best group tests run from .90 down to perhaps .70. For several individual tests and even two or three of the longest group tests, the coefficients of reliability are above .95. *See coefficient of correlation, reliability.*

> Monroe, W. S., Introduction to the Theory of Educational Measurement, p. 202f.
> Odell, C. W., Statistical Method in Education, p. 208.
> Ruch, G. M., and Stoddard, G. D., Tests and Measurements in High School Instruction, p. 355f.

Coefficient of Validity. This name is given to a coefficient of correlation between test scores and some criterion measure by which the validity of the test is being judged. *See coefficient of correlation, criterion measure, validity.*

> Odell, C. W., Statistical Method in Education, p. 57.

Column Diagram. Synonymous with histogram.

Combined Dimensions. Instead of describing each characteristic or dimension of pupils' performances separately, the directions for scoring some test papers provide for a single combined description or measure of two or in some cases three dimensions. For example, if the number of exercises done correctly is taken as the score on a uniform test, this score represents a combination of rate and accuracy. If a scaled test has a time limit short enough that pupils do not reach their limits of difficulty and if the number of exercises done correctly is taken as the score, the result is a combination of all three dimensions—rate, quality, and difficulty.

> Monroe, W. S., Introduction to the Theory of Educational Measurement, p. 130.

Comparable Measures. Measures are said to be comparable when they are expressed in terms of the same unit and with reference to the same zero point. The ordinary method of rendering the scores on two tests comparable is to change those on one to the scale used on the other. Sometimes both are changed to a common scale different from that of either. Several different methods of doing so have been recommended.

 Monroe, W. S., Introduction to the Theory of Educational Measurement, p. 211f.
 Odell, C. W., Statistical Method in Education, pp. 246, 405.

Completion Test. One of the most common forms of the new examination is the completion test. Such a test usually consists of a number of statements or sentences in each of which one or sometimes more of the important words have been omitted and are to be filled in by those being tested. Sometimes a completion test takes the form of a connected paragraph. This form of exercise is also employed in many standardized tests.

 Odell, C. W., Educational Measurement in High School, p. 491.
 Pintner, R., Intelligence Testing, p. 186.
 Ruch, G. M., and Stoddard, G. D., pp. 267, 273.

Composite Score. A composite score is the average or mean of the scores yielded by several tests after they have been expressed in terms of a common unit and from a common zero point so that the process of averaging is justified. In other words, the scores must be made comparable before being averaged. If they have not been so expressed the resulting mean is liable to have no significant meaning. The term is often limited to the mean of scores from tests in the same field.

 Monroe, W. S., Introduction to the Theory of Educational Measurement, p. 224f.

Comprehension Test. A type of mental test question found in the Binet Scale. It requires the testee to react to a situation by indicating that he understands what should be done. It is commonly used with speed in connection with measurement of reading ability.

Comprehensive Examination. A comprehensive examination is one, usually of the new type, which tests knowledge over a wide field of subject matter rather than intensively on a comparatively few topics.

Constant. In statistical tables, formulae, etc., a factor (additive, multiplicative, or exponential) which remains the same for all values of the other factors concerned.

Constant Error. A constant error is one which tends to be in the same direction for all members of a given group of pupils. Frequently also it is approximately uniform, either absolutely or relatively, for all the individuals included. The group concerned may be of any size from a portion of a class to all the children in a school system or group of systems. Constant errors do not affect the coefficient of correlation, but do affect the mean and all other measures of central tendency. Any such measures will be in error by an amount equal to the average of the constant errors in the data from which it is derived. *See variable error.*

> Monroe, W. S., Introduction to the Theory of Educational Measurement, pp. 198, 243.
> Odell, C. W., Educational Measurement in the High School, p. 69.
> Odell, C. W., Statistical Method in Education, p. 336.

Content Examination. The term content examination is used to refer to an achievement test or examination over the school subjects as distinguished from an intelligence test or a prognostic test not covering specific subjects already studied.

Control Group. In carrying on experimentation in psychology and in education it is very common to make use of two or more groups of pupils, usually though not necessarily equivalent. If there are only two groups, one of them, and if there are a larger number than two, one or more, are control groups. The pupils in control groups are subjected to the same measurements as those in the other or experimental groups but not to the experimental methods or procedures being tried out. Therefore the results in these groups serve as a basis for comparison for those obtained in the experimental groups and thus supposedly indicate how much of the gain or change produced in the latter group may have resulted from the experimental methods or procedures. *See equivalent groups method.*

Control of Testing Conditions. One of the most important essentials in the determination of norms or of scores to be compared with norms or other scores is that there be satisfactory control of the testing conditions under which the scores are obtained. These testing conditions include all factors other than pupils' abilities or knowledge which affect or determine their performances. Among the most important of these factors are the explanation of the tests to the pupils, the time allowed for their work, the form in which the tests are presented, the pupils' physical condition and emotional status, and the effort which they put forth.

> Monroe, W. S., Introduction to the Theory of Educational Measurement, p. 81f.

Correlation. The relationship between two or more series of data relating to the same individuals is called correlation. Another definition is that the method of correlation is the study of paired facts. For example, one may wish to compare pupils' marks in arithmetic with their marks in reading; that is, to compare the mark of each pupil in one subject with his mark in the other, or to compare pupils' heights and weights. Such a comparison is usually summarized by statistical methods into a single figure or index. Of such indices the coefficient of correlation is the most commonly used, but the ratio of correlation, and coefficients of rank correlation, of partial correlation, of multiple correlation, and other indices are sometimes employed. If the two series of measures or variables being compared vary together; that is, if as one increases the other also increases, the correlation is said to be positive or direct; whereas if as one increases the other tends to decrease, it is said to be negative or inverse. The coefficient of correlation and some of the other measures used range in value from $+1.00$, denoting perfect correlation, through zero, denoting no correlation at all, to -1.00, denoting perfect negative correlation. On the other hand, the ratio of correlation and several of the other measures are always positive, ranging from 1.00 down to zero, and thus do not distinguish between positive and negative correlation. It is perhaps worth noting that the existence of correlation does not at all imply causation. To illustrate, if a high correlation is found between pupils' marks in reading and their marks in arithmetic, it is not proof that one causes the other. Both may be caused by a third factor or the connection may be even more indirect than this. *See coefficient of correlation, multiple correlation, partial correlation, rank correlation*

    Odell, C. W., Statistical Method in Education, pp. 66, 143.
    Otis, A. S., Statistical Method in Educational Measurements, p. 175f.

Correlation Coefficient (r). *See coefficient of correlation.*

Correlation Graph. A correlation graph is in many ways similar to a correlation table. The difference consists in the fact that instead of containing numbers which would show the number of cases in each compartment of the table, it contains dots or other marks which show the location of the various cases on a graph constructed on the *X-* and *Y*-axes commonly used in mathematical work. *See correlation table.*

    Odell, C. W., Statistical Method in Education, p. 240.

Correlation Machine. A type of computing machine which when grouped data is used yields the various kinds of summation needed for the computation of the coefficient of correlation.

Correlation, Partial. The net relation between two traits or variables, when the influence of one or more other traits is held constant.

Correlation Table. A correlation table is a two-way or double-entry table which shows the relationship between two series of measures of the same individuals or, in other words, of a set of paired facts. If more than a small number of cases are concerned in the computation of a coefficient of correlation, the data are almost always put in this form. The scale used in measuring one of the two variables is laid out in a horizontal direction and that of the other vertically. The entry in each square or compartment of this table indicates the number of cases for which one of the measures has the value indicated by the scale value of the row, and the other measure that of the column, in which the entry occurs.

    Kelley, T. L., Interpretation of Educational Measurements, p. 158f.
    Odell, C. W., Statistical Method in Education, p. 162.

Counseling. The activity where the available facts are gathered together and the individual's experiences are focused upon a specific problem to aid him in their solution. Counseling should be aimed at the progressive development of the individual so that he solves his own problems with a minimum of assistance.

    Jones, A. J., Principles of Guidance, p. 276.

Counselor. In the general sense, any person who helps other individuals in solving their problems of adjustment. A counselor is often more properly conceived as a trained specialist who has certain definite functions to perform in a guidance program. Today the former connotation is more frequently used.

    Jones, A. J., Principles of Guidance, pp. 258, 264, 271–78, 284, 297, 299, 374, 396, 398, 402, 418.

Criterion. The term criterion is applied to any principle, law, fact, or other standard by which validity may be determined. This includes not merely the validity of a test or scale but also of the selection of cases or items, of a basis of comparison, a statement of a problem, an assumption, a method of procedure, or any other step involved in research.

> Monroe, W. S., Introduction to the Theory of Educational Measurement, p. 183f.
> Ruch, G. M., and Stoddard, G. D., Tests and Measurements in High School Instruction, p. 45f.

Criterion Measure. A criterion measure is any measure which may be used as a basis for comparison or correlation to determine the validity of the scores yielded by a given test. Teachers' estimates of achievement and sometimes of intelligence, school marks, school grade, the composite scores from a number of tests, and sometimes the scores from a single other test, are among the criterion measures most commonly used. It should perhaps be noted that for group tests of intelligence a very common criterion measure has been the Stanford Revision of the Binet-Simon Scale.

> Monroe, W. S., Introduction to the Theory of Educational Measurement, p. 221f.

Critical Attitude. This attitude requires that assumptions, data, conclusions, and all other activities or procedures be subject to critical scrutiny to determine their validity for the purposes for which they are employed. To state it differently, the critical attitude requires that an investigator have an unprejudiced attitude and carefully weigh all the evidence at hand before arriving at any conclusion. It also requires that the conclusions reached be considered more or less tentative rather than final and always subject to revision in the light of any fresh evidence which appears to justify revision. *See Scientific.*

Cross-Out Test. This name has been applied to various varieties of the new examination in which pupils are required to cross out certain items. Probably its most frequent application has been to the form of association or multiple-answer test in which several terms are given and the one or perhaps more not connected with a given term or similar to the majority are to be crossed out. It is also used in a number of standardized tests.

Crude Data. Data are said to be crude when they are not highly exact or accurate but are merely comparatively rough approximations. This condition is usually due to the use of measuring instruments that have rather large units or are in some other way relatively unrefined. Thus if pupils' heights are measured with a foot-rule containing no divisions, the resulting measurements are very crude. If heights are measured with a ruler divided into inches but not into fractions of inches the resulting measurements are still somewhat crude.

Crude Score. This expression is used in two slightly different ways. In one the adjective crude has the same meaning as in the expression crude data explained just above. In the other crude score may be considered as synonymous with raw score.

C-Scale. The C-scale is similar to the T-scale, the chief difference being that the unit used is .1 quartile deviation instead of .1 standard deviation. The scale extends the same distance as the T-scale; that is, from five standard deviations below the mean to five above the mean, and therefore since the quartile deviation is only about two-thirds the standard deviation, it is composed of 148 units instead of the 100 of the T-scale. Comparatively few tests provide for the use of the C-scale. *See T-scale.*

Odell, C. W., Educational Measurement in High School, p. 448.

C-Score. A score given according to the C-scale. The range of such scores is from zero through 74, the average, up to 148. Such a score indicates the point on the scale at which the difficulty is such that the pupil receiving this score can respond correctly to just half the exercises of that difficulty.

Odell, C. W., Educational Measurement in High School, p. 448.

Cumulative Frequency Curve. Synonymous with ogive.

Cumulative Frequency Table. A cumulative frequency table is one in which the frequencies or entries indicate the total number of cases either in and below, or in and above, as the case may be, the given class. The former is most common. Such a table is generally constructed from an ordinary frequency table. To make a cumulative table indicating the total number of cases in and below, the frequencies in an ordinary frequency table are summed up to and including each class to obtain the cumulative frequency for that class. For example, if there are two cases in the lowest class, three in the next to the lowest and six in the next, the cumulative frequency for the latter is eleven, found by adding two, three, and six. For a cumulative table showing the number of cases in and above the ordinary frequencies are summed down to and including each class to yield the cumulative frequency for it.

Odell, C. W., Statistical Methods in Education, p. 28.

Cumulative Records. Reports or complete case histories are usually given. The term may be used in two senses. It may be a record of all available significant information about an individual at a specific time or it may cover a longer period in the life of the individual. It is often thought that when facts are considered in the light of each other, they are more reliable.

Jones, A. J., Principles of Guidance, pp. 221–233.

Curving Fitting or Smoothing. A process of finding the regular or smooth curve which most closely approximates a series of measurements. Fitting may be by eye or by elaborate mathematical computations.

Curvilinear Relationship. The term curvilinear is used in contrast to rectilinear to apply to cases in which the best graphic representation of the relationship between two variables is a curved line rather than a straight line. That line of relationship from which the total deviation or departure of the measures is the least is considered the best fitting line. If the departure from a straight and a curved line is the same, the former is preferred. The most common, indeed practically the only, expression employed as an index of curvilinear relationship is the ratio of correlation. *See ratio of correlation.*

Odell, C. W., Statistical Method in Education, p. 147, 250, 293, 307.

Cycle Test. A cycle test consists of exercises or items differing in difficulty or perhaps in form or kind, but so arranged that the variations occur in cycles. For example, a cycle of four might be used, in which case the first, fifth, ninth, and so forth exercises would be similar; likewise the second, sixth, tenth, and so forth would be similar; also the third, seventh, eleventh, and so forth. A cycle test may be treated as a uniform test as regards both administration and scoring without introducing serious errors. Its use is to be recommended when it is desired to include within a single test exercises of several levels of difficulty or of several different sorts. This procedure makes sure that all pupils attempt some of each difficulty or sort.

D

D. This letter is used as an abbreviation in several different connections. Perhaps the most common of these is that D is used for difference in one method of rank correlation. The difference referred to is that between the rank of a case in one series of measures and its rank in the other. D is also frequently used as an abbreviation for the 10–90 percentile range. Sometimes D is the abbreviation for decile, but Dec. is better used in this connection.

Data. The information employed in educational and psychological research is not limited to collections of statistical facts, but also includes historical facts, principles, opinions, and items of various other sorts. Such information is expressed in terms of numerical scores.

Dean. One whose job is to correlate the efforts of parents, community agents, teachers, etc. in the problem of educational, social, and personal adjustment of school pupils. Sometimes the term is used synonymous with "counselor" or "advisor".

Jones, A. J., Principles of Guidance, p. 398.

Dec. Abbreviation for decile. The subscripts 1, 2, and so on up to 9 are used to indicate the first decile, second decile, and so on up to the ninth.

Decile. The deciles are the points which divide the total number of cases contained in a frequency distribution into ten equal parts; that is, into ten parts each of which contains the same number of cases. Thus $\frac{1}{10}$ of all the cases lie at or below the first decile and $\frac{9}{10}$ at or above it, etc. Occasionally the term decile is also applied to one of the ten parts mentioned above.

Odell, C. W., Statistical Method in Education, p. 113.

Derived Measure. A derived measure is one which is derived or computed from the original measures obtained. Among the most common derived measures are the mean, the median, the mode, the quartile deviation, the standard deviation, the mean deviation, the probable error, the coefficient of correlation, the ratio of correlation, and the coefficient of regression. Derived measure is also sometimes used as synonymous with derived score or transmuted measure.

Derived Score. Except by chance, two or more tests do not yield point scores expressed in terms of the same unit or from the same zero point. Therefore a number of proposals have been made looking to the calculation and use of scores which describe pupils' performances in terms of a unit and zero point constant for all tests or at least for a large number of tests. Such scores are called derived scores. They include age scores, grade scores, quotient scores, percentile scores, T-scores, and others.

    Monroe, W. S., DeVoss, J. C., and Kelly, F. J., Educational Tests and Measurements, p. 380f.
    Symonds, P., Measurement in Secondary Education, p. 310f.

Deviation. The spread or scatter of a set of measures about a point, which is almost always a measure of central tendency—that is, an average—is called deviation. It is commonly measured by any one of several measures of deviation or variability each of which yields a summary statement from a slightly different standpoint. Such measures as the range, the mean deviation, the median deviation, the quartile deviation, the standard deviation, are illustrations.

    Odell, C. W., Statistical Method in Education, pp. 69, 115.

Deviation, Average. *See mean deviation.*

Deviation, Quartile. One-half the difference between the 25th and the 75th percentiles in a frequency distribution of measures.

Deviation, Standard. *See standard deviation.*

Diagnosis. By general diagnosis we mean any procedure that may be used to secure general information regarding the educational status of a pupil or of a class.

    Brueckner, L. J., and Melby, E. O., Diagnostic and Remedial Teaching, p. 124.
    Odell, C. W., Educational Measurement in High School, p. 545.

Diagnostic Test. A diagnostic test is one which yields detailed information concerning pupils' achievement in one or perhaps more relatively restricted fields. This type of measuring instrument frequently consists of several sub-tests which yield separate measures of pupils' achievements in a variety of fields. The primary purpose of diagnostic tests is to point out the specific weaknesses or strengths of pupils as a basis for remedial suggestions.

    Brueckner, L. J., and Melby, E. O., Diagnostic and Remedial Teaching, p. 73.
    Monroe, W. S., Introduction to the Theory of Educational Measurement, p. 40.
    Orleans, J. S., Measurement in Education, pp. 155, 387.
    Ruch, G. M., and Stoddard, G. D., Tests and Measurements in High School Instruction, pp. 64, 65.

Difficulty. Difficulty is one of the three characteristics or dimensions of pupils' performances. It has been defined as that characteristic of an exercise which when present in a large degree causes a large per cent of incorrect responses. In other words, the degree of difficulty of an exercise is determined by the per cent of incorrect responses obtained when it is given to a large number of pupils. If the point of zero difficulty is determined and if certain assumptions are made concerning the distribution of ability of the group of pupils to whom an exercise is given, the degree of difficulty of an exercise can be expressed in terms of a measure of the variability of this distribution of ability. This unit is the difference in difficulty between two exercises each of which is answered correctly by a certain given per cent of pupils, the two given per cents of course being different. The median deviation, usually incorrectly called the probable error, and the standard deviation are the two units most commonly used for this purpose. Thus the difficulty of an exercise may be described as being 1.4 P.E., 2.5 P.E., 1.27σ, and so forth.

    Monroe, W. S., Introduction to the Theory of Educational Measurement, pp. 61f.
    Odell, C. W., Educational Measurement in the High School, p. 19.

Difficulty Scale. A scale in which the items are arranged in order of difficulty. The relative difficulty of each item is determined experimentally by finding the per cent of persons in a large group who are able to solve each problem correctly.

Difficulty Score. A difficulty score is a statement of the highest level of difficulty on which a pupil has responded to the exercises with a specified or standard degree of accuracy. Sometimes 100 per cent accuracy is required, sometimes 50 per cent accuracy, and occasionally some other per cent. Such a score is yielded only by scaled tests. *See difficulty.*

> Monroe, W. S., Introduction to the Theory of Educational Measurement, pp. 94f., 118f.
> Odell, C. W., Educational Measurement in the High School, pp. 19, 20.

Direct Correlation. Synonymous with positive correlation.

Directions Test. A directions test is one which measures the ability of pupils to carry out directions as given. Such a test is found as a part of a number of intelligence tests.

> Freeman, F. N., Mental Tests, p. 262.
> Pintner, R., Intelligence Testing, p. 186.

Director of Guidance. A person who devotes all or nearly all of his time to the problems of guidance. One on whom the direct responsibility for carrying out such activity is placed. This special position is created more in the large school, while in a smaller organization a principal or class room teacher may devote part of his or her time to the program. In either case discipline should not be connected with this task.

> Jones, A. J., Principles of Guidance, p. 412, 414–15, 431.

Discrimination. A test is said to possess satisfactory discrimination when the scores earned upon it by pupils who are known to differ in ability vary in accord with these known differences. Thus a test that is too easy lacks discrimination because a number of pupils make perfect scores, and one that is too hard lacks it because a number of pupils make zero scores. *See undistributed scores.*

> Monroe, W. S., Introduction to the Theory of Educational Measurement, p. 219f.

Discussion Examination. Synonymous with traditional examination.

Dispersion. Synonymous with deviation.

Distribution. In statistics an arrangement which shows the frequency of occurrence of each successive value or range of values.

> Otis, A. S., Statistical Method in Educational Measurements, p. 14.

Division. As applied to tests, this is usually synonymous with *part*.

Dotting Test. A form of psychological test of speed and accuracy of voluntary movement in which the person tested is directed to make a series of dots as rapidly as possible. The score on such a test is usually expressed in terms of speed and accuracy scores.

Duplicate Form. Most standardized tests possess two or more forms usually called Form A, Form B, and so forth, or Form 1, Form 2, and so forth. These forms consist of exercises alike in form and kind, though not identical. In almost all cases such duplicate forms have been constructed with the intention that they shall be of equivalent difficulty, but this result has not always been attained. Such forms are used when a test must be repeated, in order to avoid practice effect or to avoid pupils' cheating when proper seating conditions can not be arranged.

>Monroe, W. S., Introduction to the Theory of Educational Measurements, p. 169f.
>Odell, C. W., Educational Measurement in the High School, p. 74.
>Ruch, G. M., and Stoddard, G. D., Tests and Measurements in High School Instruction, p. 65.

E

E. A. Abbreviation for educational age.
E. Q. Abbreviation for educational quotient.
E. R. Abbreviation for educational ratio.

Educational Age (E. A.). This expression is almost but not quite synonymous with achievement age. It differs in that it is ordinarily applied only to a pupil's average standing in a number of school subjects expressed in terms of an age score, whereas achievement age may refer to a single subject or the average of several. *See achievement age, subject age.*

>Brueckner, L. J., and Melby, E. O., Diagnostic and Remedial Teaching, p. 101.
>Greene, H. A. and Jorgensen, A. N., Use and Interpretation of High School Tests, p. 223.
>Orleans, J. S., Measurement in Education, p. 222.
>Otis, A. S., Statistical Method in Educational Measurements, p. 444.

Educational Guidance. As distinguished from vocational guidance, educational guidance is the advising and directing of pupils in the choice of subjects and other matters connected with his further education and not in regard to the choice of a vocation or occupation. These two types of guidance are, however, closely related, and frequently, perhaps usually, must be considered together because of this inter-relationship.

Odell, C. W., Educational Measurement in the High School, p. 520.
Jones, A. J., Principles of Guidance, pp. 287–314.

Educational Objectives, Agreement With. In the selection of exercises or items to be included in a test and of subject matter to be included in a course or curriculum, it is desirable to examine such exercise items, or subject matter with reference to their agreement with educational objectives. For example, in the construction of his spelling scale, Ayres selected certain words on the basis of their frequency of use in adult correspondence. Charters studied the language errors most commonly made by children and not only incorporated these into his language and grammar tests but also made them the basis of a course of study in this subject. In other cases the consensus of opinion of competent persons, or what amounts to almost the same thing, frequency of occurrence in textbooks, has been employed as a guide in selection.

Monroe, W. S., Introduction to the Theory of Educational Measurement, p. 89f.

Educational Quotient (E. Q.). The quotient obtained by dividing a pupil's educational age by his chronological age has been called his educational quotient. That is,

$$E.\ Q. = \frac{E.\ A.}{C.\ A.}.$$

Such a quotient shows a pupil's average standing in a number of school subjects as compared with the average of pupils of his chronological age. Educational quotients may also be used to express a pupil's standing in specific subjects such as reading, etc., measured by the New Stanford Achievement Test Battery, or any other battery test. *See achievement quotient, subject quotient.*

Greene, H. A., and Jorgensen, A. N., Use and Interpretation of High School Tests, p. 240.
McCall, W. A., How to Measure in Education, p. 36f.
Monroe, W. S., Introduction to the Theory of Educational Measurement, p. 156f.
Odell, C. W., Educational Measurement in the High School, p. 446.
Orleans, J. S., Measurement in Education, pp. 222, 367.

Educational Ratio (E. R.). Some of those who have advocated that the result obtained by dividing a pupil's educational age by his chronological age be called his educational quotient have also proposed that his educational age divided by his mental age be called his educational ratio. The same result can be obtained by dividing the educational quotient by the intelligence quotient. An educational ratio in this sense is, therefore, synonymous with an achievement quotient in its usual sense if that achievement quotient is the average of quotients in several different subjects. *See achievement quotient.*

Educational Test. Synonymous with achievement test.

Empirical Test. An empirical test is a test chosen through the trial and error method. A number of tests are tried out, usually without any very strong theoretical reason why they, rather than others, should be considered, and the one or ones which appear most useful for the purpose in mind selected. This method of choosing tests has probably received more use in connection with vocational prognosis or prediction of aptitude than in any other field.

Equivalent Form. If two or more duplicate forms which have been prepared for many standardized tests yield equal or equivalent scores, they are said to be equivalent. In very few, if any, cases is the equivalence perfect. *See duplicate form, form.*

    Monroe, W. S., Introduction to the Theory of Educational Measurement, p. 169f.
    Odell, C. W., Educational Measurement in the High School, p. 74.
    Ruch, G. M., and Stoddard, G. D., Tests and Measurements in High School Instruction, p. 65.

Equivalent Groups Method. This is a method of educational experimentation in which two or more equivalent groups of pupils are used. Different procedures or methods are employed in the two or more groups and the comparison of results at the end of the experiment offers evidence concerning the relative merits of these procedures or methods. In general, groups are considered equivalent when their means and variabilities are the same. It is desirable and for some purposes necessary, however, that the pupils in one group match those in another, taken pair by pair.

Error. There are a number of kinds of errors present in educational data. In most instances their magnitude and number can be determined approximately, but not for any particular individual. *See constant error, error of estimate, error of measurement, error of sampling, variable error.*

    Odell, C. W., Educational Measurement in the High School, pp. 62, 65 592.
    Odell, C. W., Statistical Method in Education, pp. 7, 326.

Error of Estimate. Errors of estimate are those errors involved in estimating the values of one variable from those of another by the use of the regression equation. For example, if the scores of number of pupils upon an intelligence test and their average school marks have been correlated and the regression obtained, the differences between the estimates of school marks based upon intelligence test scores and the marks actually assigned are errors of estimate. Also if school marks are known and intelligence test scores estimated from them, the differences between estimated and actual scores are errors of estimate. Such errors are usually measured by the standard or probable error of estimate.

> Monroe, W. S., Introduction to the Theory of Educational Measurement, pp. 199f., 350f.
> Odell, C. W., Statistical Method in Education, p. 363.
> Odell, C. W., Educational Measurement in the High School, p. 592.

Error of Measurement. Errors of measurement are similar to errors of estimate, but differ in that whereas the latter are involved in estimating one actual or obtained score from another, errors of measurement are those involved in estimating true scores from a series of actual scores. For example, if two equivalent forms of a reading test have been given, the errors involved in estimating Form 2 scores from Form 1 scores, or vice versa, are errors of estimate whereas those involved in estimating true scores from either Form 1 or Form 2 scores are errors of measurement.

> Monroe, W. S., Introduction to the Theory of Educational Measurement, pp. 207f., 354f.
> Odell, C. W., Educational Measurement in the High School, pp. 62, 65, 592.
> Odell, C. W., Statistical Method in Education, pp. 326, 366.

Error of Sampling. Errors of sampling occur in derived measures and are due to the fact that such measures are frequently calculated from a limited number of cases chosen as being representative of a larger group or population. In many cases it is either impossible or impracticable to utilize all cases of the sort being dealt with. For example, if one desires to make a study of ten-year-old boys he must do so by using a selected sample of boys of that age, and derived measures computed from this sample contain errors of sampling. If, as is generally assumed, the sample is chosen without bias, the errors in the derived measures will be smaller, the larger the sample. Their magnitude decreases in inverse ratio to the square root of the number of cases; therefore since 200 is four times 50 and the square root of four is two, the average magnitude of the errors present in derived measures obtained from a sample of 200 individuals would be only one-half as great as in those obtained from 50 individuals. Errors of sampling are commonly described by stating the probable or the standard error of the derived measure in question. *See random sample, sampling.*

> Monroe, C. W., Introduction to the Theory of Educational Measurement, p. 330.
>
> Odell, C. W., Statistical Method in Education, p. 326.

Essay Examination. Synonymous with traditional examination.

Eta (η). Abbreviation for the ratio of correlation.

Examination. 1. An evaluation by means of tests and other data of an individual's status with respect to one or more specific fields of ability, achievement, or skill; or with respect to other psychological traits.

2. (Statistical) Systematic inspection of collected data with a view to judging their value.

Exercise. An exercise is a structural unit of a test, or in other words, a unit governed by a single set of directions. Some of the simpler types of exercises merely call for a word to be spelled, an arithmetical example to be worked, or a question to be answered. Others are more complex. Some consist of a number of items. A test usually consists of at least several exercises, but occasionally of a single long one.

> Green, H. A., and Jorgensen, A. N., Use and Interpretation of High School Tests, pp. 73, 75.
>
> Monroe, W. S., Introduction to the Theory of Educational Measurement, pp. 56f., 89f.

Experimental Coefficient. It has been suggested that instead of comparing the difference between two means or other derived measures directly with the probable or standard error of the difference in order to determine its reliability, a formula yielding what is known as the experimental coefficient be used for this purpose. This formula requires merely that the difference be divided by 2.78 times the standard error of the difference. In other words,

$$\text{Exp. Coef.} = \frac{\text{Diff.}}{2.78\sigma \text{ diff.}}.$$

The resulting experimental coefficient is interpreted by means of a table of chances which shows how likely it is that the difference in question is significant. The smaller the experimental coefficient, the smaller are the chances that it is so. An experimental coefficient of 1.0 is generally accepted as practical certainty.

McCall, W. A., How to Measure in Education, p. 404f.
Odell, C. W., Statistical Methods in Education, p. 355.

Experimental Factor. The factor or element in the situation with which one is experimenting is sometimes called the experimental factor. Sometimes only one such factor is involved, sometimes more than one.

Experimental Group. One of the most common methods of educational experimentation involves the use of two or more groups of pupils. The one or more of these in which the experimental procedures or methods are employed are generally called experimental groups in contrast with the others which merely serve for checking results and are called control or check groups. It is usually desirable that the experimental and the control groups be equivalent, but it is often satisfactory if they are not provided the differences between them are known and measured. *See equivalent groups method.*

Experimentation. Although experimentation is only one of the methods of educational research, it has probably received the major part of the attention and emphasis in this general field within recent years. It may be defined as that method which tests theory by a process of trying it out and evaluating the results obtained. Its purpose is to evaluate some one or more of the factors which enter into the educational process. Experimentation should begin with the definition of a problem followed by the setting up of conditions and the carrying out of procedures which contribute to the solution of the problem. The experimenter should maintain and apply the critical or scientific attitude.

Extra-Class Activities. Out of class activities which are a part of a pupil's school program and which should be a part of any pupil's record. These involve little formalized activity and give the student a larger degree of freedom.

Jones, A. J., Principles of Guidance, pp. 131-136.

F

f. Abbreviation for frequency.

Fables Test. A test in which the person tested is asked to tell what lesson a fable, which is read to him or by him, is intended to teach. This test is found in the Stanford Revision of the Binet-Simon Scale.

Fact-Finding Study. A fact-finding study is one in which the main purpose is to determine and collect facts. Although such studies are important and necessary, they cannot be said to be complete educational research. The data found in this manner must be such that it can be interpreted and classified.

Factor Theory. A theory based on empirical and statistical findings seeking to explain intelligence as a measurable phenomenon in terms of relations among capacities which vary in number in extensity, and in organization.

    Freeman, F. N., Mental Tests, pp. 60, 476–479.
    Pintner, R., Intelligence Testing, pp. 63–68.

First Quartile (Q_1). The first quartile is that point on the scale of measurement used in connection with any distribution or series of measurements at or below which one-fourth and at or above which three-fourths of the measures fall.

$$Q_1 = 1 + \frac{\frac{N}{4} - S}{f}.$$

See quartile.

    Greene, H. A., and Jorgensen, A. N., Use and Interpretation of High School Tests, p. 175.
    Odell, C. W., Educational Measurement in the High School, pp. 562, 598.
    Odell, C. W., Statistical Method in Education, p. 105.
    Otis, A. S., Statistical Method in Educational Measurements, p. 33.

Foot-Rule Correlation (R). One of the two common methods of securing rank correlation is the foot-rule method, which may be applied with comparative ease. In the foot-rule formula, which originated with Spearman, the symbol for correlation is R, and the value of R is determined by the differences between the ranks of the measures in the corresponding pairs.

>McCall, W. A., How to Measure in Education, pp. 391, 392, 393.
>Odell, C. W., Educational Measurement in the High School, p. 588.
>Odell, C. W., Statistical Method in Education, p. 226.
>Otis, A. S., Statistical Method in Educational Measurements, p. 210.

Fore-Exercise. A fore-exercise is a preliminary or trial test which has for its purpose acquainting the pupils with the character of the exercises which they are asked to do in the real test. In administering a test the person doing so should usually see to it that the pupils make the correct responses on the fore-exercises. The pupils' performances thereon are not included in computing their scores. A good illustration of such exercises is found in the National Intelligence Test or the Otis Self-Administering Test of Intelligence.

>Odell, C. W., Educational Measurement in the High School, p. 68.

Form. This term has come to be generally used in the sense of the duplicate forms of tests. A test is said to have two or more forms when it has two or more copies consisting of similar but not identical exercises or material. In a very few cases the word form has been used as synonymous with part, division, or even test. That is to say that Form 1 might be used to indicate the portion of the test for the lower grades, Form 2 for the upper grades. This usage is, however, so rare as to be practically negligible.

>Greene, H. A., and Jorgensen, A. N., Use and Interpretation of High School Tests, pp. 140–142.
>Odell, C. W., Educational Measurement in High School, p. 74.
>Orleans, J. S., Measurement in Education, p. 70.
>Symonds, P., Measurement in Secondary Education, pp. 305–306.

Form-Board. This term is applied to numerous kinds of performance tests in which blocks of wood are fitted into a board with depressions of various sizes and shapes, beads are arranged in patterns, or puzzle types of materials are assembled in proper form. Usually the pupil's responses on such a test are scored in regard to both speed and accuracy.

>Freeman, F. N., Mental Tests, p. 124.
>Pintner, R., Intelligence Testing, pp. 160–164.

Form-Board Test. A type of task in which the testee is required to place blocks of different shapes, sizes, colors, or designs in appropriate insets in a board, the score being expressed in terms of time, errors, or both. *See form-board.*

    Freeman, F. N., Mental Tests, p. 124.
    Pintner, R., Intelligence Testing, pp. 160–164.

Frequency. This term when used as a noun refers to the number of measures or scores in a class, or in other words, to an entry in a frequency or correlation table. For example, if in a table of students' I. Q.'s by five-point intervals, there are ten cases of persons with I. Q.'s from 90 up to but not including 100, the frequency in this class is said to be 10. *See frequency curve, frequency polygon, frequency table.*

    Greene, H. A., and Jorgensen, A. N., Use and Interpretation of High School Tests, pp. 152, 153.
    McCall, W. A., How to Measure in Education, pp. 359, 364.
    Odell, C. W., Educational Measurement in the High School, p. 555.
    Odell, C. W., Statistical Method in Education, p. 17.
    Otis, A. S., Statistical Method in Educational Measurements, p. 15.
    Symonds, P., Measurement in Secondary Education, p. 550.

Frequency Curve. This expression is used in two senses. In the wider sense a frequency curve is any sort of curve or graph which represents a distribution of measures or scores. The three common varieties thereof are the smooth frequency curve, the histogram, and the frequency polygon. All of these are commonly drawn so that the scale of measurement by which the cases included are measured is laid out horizontally, and the scale showing the number of cases or frequencies, vertically. In its narrower sense it refers to a smooth curve which represents a distribution of measures. It is drawn by constructing a smooth curve through points located as for a frequency polygon. *Also see normal frequency curve.*

    McCall, W. A., How to Measure in Education, pp. 359, 364.
    Odell, C. W., Statistical Method in Education, p. 17.
    Otis, A. S., Statistical Method in Educational Measurements, p. 15.

Frequency Distribution. Synonymous with frequency table.

Frequency Polygon. A frequency polygon is one of the three common types of graphs used to represent a distribution of measures. It is constructed by determining and connecting with straight lines a series of points each one of which is directly above the midpoint of a class interval, and at a height equal to the frequency in the class.

> Odell, C. W., Statistical Method in Education, pp. 37, 422.
> Symonds, P., Measurement in Secondary Education, p. 240.

Frequency Table. A frequency table consists of one column which indicates the limits of the various classes into which the individual cases included have been grouped and a second which shows the number or frequency of cases in each class or grouping. Such a table is illustrated by the columns at the right. The first of these columns designates the various class intervals and the second gives the frequency or number of cases in each. In this example the class intervals are designated in the most common way; that is, by giving the lower limit only of each class. It is then understood that a given class includes all measures from the given lower limit up to the lower limit of the next class. For example, the first class in the table—that is, the one at the bottom—includes all cases having magnitudes of from zero up to but not including 10; the next one all those from 10 up to but not including 20, and so on. The figures in the second column show that the frequency in the 0-up-to-but-not-including-10 class is one, and so forth.

```
80 — 2
70 — 4
60 — 5
50 — 6
40 — 9
30 — 7
20 — 5
10 — 2
 0 — 1
   —
N = 41
```

> Greene, H. A., and Jorgensen, A. N., Use and Interpretation of High School Tests, pp. 152, 153.
> Odell, C. W., Statistical Method in Education, p. 17.

Frequency Tabulation. Synonymous with frequency table.

Function. As used in the field of education function may be considered as synonymous with purpose or aim. The term is frequently employed in connection with standardized tests. The function of such a test is described by a statement of the type of information concerning this ability which it will yield. This statement is usually made in the test manual but may often be indicated by the title of the test, such as Pressey Diagnostic Test in English Composition, or Orleans Algebra Prognosis.

> Monroe, W. S., Introduction to the Theory of Educational Measurement, p. 18f.

Functional Relation. A functional relation is said to exist between two variables if a change in one produces a corresponding proportional change in the other. The relation between the two variables may be very simple, or it may be decidedly complex and require a considerable amount of computation to determine one from the other. The former, a very simple functional relation, may be illustrated by such an equation as $x = 6y$, which merely means that any change in y is accompanied by a corresponding change 6 times as great in x. A more complex functional relation is indicated by such an equation as

$$x = \sqrt[3]{\frac{y}{2}}.$$

This equation signifies that as y is changed in a given ratio, x changes correspondingly according to the cube root of that ratio divided by two. One of the primary assumptions in much if not all educational measurement is that pupils' performances sustain a constant functional relation to the abilities which are being measured.

    Monroe, W. S., Introduction to the Theory of Educational Measurements, pp. 22, 24.

G

g. Abbreviation for gain in connection with one method of computing rank correlation.

G. Sometimes used as abbreviation for geometric mean.

G. A. Abbreviation for guessed average.

G Factor (General Factor). A psychoneural element, or determiner, according to the two-factor theory of intelligence, which is fundamental to all correlated abilities for the same person, as distinguished from the specific *s factors* which vary in different activities. See *factor theory*.

    Freeman, F. N., Mental Tests, pp. 60, 476–479.
    Pintner, R., Intelligence Testing, pp. 63–68.

General Intelligence Test. A test which is designed to measure general intelligence or intellectual capacity is usually called a general intelligence test in contrast with a test designed to measure actual ability or achievement in some school subject. General intellectual capacity may be defined as that mental capacity which supposedly may be applied in any field of intellectual endeavor. In one sense intelligence is a person's ability to adjust to a situation and to readjust when the situation changes. The term mental alertness has often been suggested for such tests. An intelligence test usually consists of various types of test materials or test exercises intended to measure various aspects of motor ability. It is assumed that the average or combined score from a number of such kinds of exercises yields a fairly accurate measure of general intelligence.

> Freeman, F. N., Mental Tests, p. 476f.
> Greene, H. A., and Jorgensen, A. N., Use and Interpretation of High School Tests, pp. 263-270.
> Kelley, T. L., Interpretation of Educational Measurements, pp. 4, 116f.
> Monroe, W. S., DeVoss, J. C., and Kelly, F. J., Educational Tests and Measurements, p. 332f.
> Odell, C. W., Educational Measurement in the High School, pp. 22, 300.
> Orleans, J. S., Measurement in Education, p. 66.
> Pintner, R., Intelligence Testing (entire).

General Survey Test. A general survey test is usually composed of a number of tests or sub-tests each of which covers a different school subject or field of subject matter. Occasionally, however, the term is applied to a test in a single school subject which contains a number of parts covering different phases of the subject. The function of such a test is to yield a general or average measure of pupils' achievements over a comparatively wide field. Ordinarily the scores yielded by the different portions of a general survey test are combined into a single score. Such scores are valuable for determining the general efficiency of a school or teacher, but are rarely of much help in diagnostic and individual work. Scores are usually stated in terms of educational age or school grade-placement. The Metropolitan or the New Stanford Achievement Test are good examples of a general survey test.

> Brueckner, L. J., and Melby, E. O., Diagnostic and Remedial Teaching, p. 71.
> Orleans, J. S., Measurement in Education, p. 104.
> Monroe, W. S., DeVoss, J. C., and Kelly, F. J., Educational Tests and Measurements, p. 377f.
> Ruch, G. M., and Stoddard, G. D., Tests and Measurements in High School Instruction, p. 200f.

Genius. A person of very superior mental ability; especially one of superior power of invention or origination of any kind, or of execution of some special form, such as music, art, or mechanics. The term has no special technical meaning, but has occasionally been defined as equivalent to an intelligence quotient (I. Q.) of 140 or above.

Pintner, R., Intelligence Testing, pp. 350–372.

Geometric Mean (G. M., G., or M.). This mean is used in dealing with rates of increase. It is the nth root of the product of n measures and therefore must usually be found by the use of logarithms.

Odell, C. W., Statistical Method in Education, pp. 91, 97, 102.
Otis, A. S., Statistical Method in Educational Measurements, p. 7.

G. M. Abbreviation for geometric mean, also sometimes for guessed mean, more commonly known as assumed mean.

Grade. The term is commonly used in two distinct senses. One of these is in such expressions as first grade, second grade, seventh grade, etc., to refer to the various stages of advancement in school or units of school organization. The term is also frequently employed to refer to ratings given to pupils in such expressions as a grade of 85 per cent or a grade of B. It is decidedly preferable, however, to use the word mark in this second sense and to limit grade to the first meaning given, thus avoiding possible confusion resulting from its double use.

Grade Norm. A grade norm is a statement of the achievement or sometimes capacity of pupils in a particular grade. The average or median score of a large number of pupils in a single grade is usually taken as the norm for that grade though rarely some other point is used. Grade norms are ordinarily based upon the supposition that a school system contains eight elementary grades and four years of high-school work; therefore if used for comparative purposes in connection with a system which has a different organization, adjustments are necessary. There is no uniformity as to the time of year for which grade norms are given so that this fact should always be stated. Some tests give grade norms for each month of the school year and others give norms at the end of half years, such as in February or June. *See norm.*

Brueckner, L. J., and Melby, E. O., Diagnostic and Remedial Teaching, p. 71.
Freeman, F. N., Mental Tests, p. 294f.
McCall, W. A., How to Measure in Education, pp. 32–37.
Monroe, W. S., Introduction to the Theory of Educational Measurement, p. 161f.
Ruch, G. M., and Stoddard, G. D., Tests and Measurements in High School Instruction, p. 344f.

Grade Scale. A scale for measuring ability or growth in which the units of measurement are the successive grade norms.
    McCall, W. A., How to Measure in Education, pp. 258–263.

Graphic Rating Scale. A method for obtaining and recording a judgment concerning the degree to which a person possesses a specified trait or characteristic, by marking an appropriate position between the two extremes of a line that represents the possible range of degrees of the trait.
    Orleans, J. S., Measurement in Education, p. 158.
    Otis, A. S., Statistical Method in Educational Measurements, p. 286.
    Symonds, P., Measurement in Secondary Education, pp. 344, 345.
    Ruch, G. M., and Stoddard, G. D., Tests and Measurements in High School Instruction, pp. 312–317.

Grouping. This term refers to the classifying or collecting of single measures into classes or groups so that instead of a simple or ungrouped series, a frequency table is formed. This term is also used in connection with the formation of sections or divisions of grades or classes. *See homogeneous grouping.*
    Greene, H. A., and Jorgensen, A. N., Use and Interpretation of High School Tests, pp. 151–158.
    Kelley, T. L., Interpretation of Educational Measurements, p. 161.
    Odell, C. W., Statistical Method in Education, pp. 14, 18.
    Odell, C. W., Educational Measurement in the High School, p. 516.
    Otis, A. S., Statistical Method in Educational Measurements, p. 194.

Group Test. A test which can be given to a number of individuals at the same time and by the same examiner is called a group test. Almost all standardize tests are group tests, the chief exceptions being those in oral reading and a few individual ones in intelligence.
    Freeman, F. N., Mental Tests, p. 164f.
    Greene, H. A., and Jorgensen, A. N., Use and Interpretation of High School Tests, p. 265.
    Pintner, R., Intelligence Testing, pp. 180–221.

Guessed Average (G. A.). Synonymous with assumed mean, which is a better term.

Guidance. *See educational guidance, vocational guidance.*

H

Halo Effect. A tendency, when estimating or rating a person with respect to a certain trait or ability, to be influenced by an estimate of some other trait or by one's general impression of the person. This is an important source of error and can be offset only by making the rating as objective and impersonal as possible.

    Odell, C. W., Educational Measurement in the High School, p. 416.
    Symonds, P., Measurement in Secondary Education, p. 348.

Histogram. A histogram or column diagram is one of the three common types of frequency curves. It may be thought of as composed of a series of rectangles one of which is erected above each class interval. The width of each rectangle represents the width of the class interval and its height the number of cases or frequencies in the class. Usually the dividing lines between the rectangles are not shown. *See frequency curve.*

    Odell, C. W., Statistical Method in Education, p. 34, 41, 422.
    Otis, A. S., Statistical Method in Educational Measurements, p. 31f.

Homeroom Guidance. The guidance which is possible because of the homeroom situation. Homerooms are needed because of a desire for better teacher-pupil contacts. This type of guidance is performed by the homeroom teacher.

    Jones, A. J., Principles of Guidance, p. 278-284, 374, 389.

Homogeneous Grouping. A term usually used in connection with the classification of pupils, in which groups are arranged according to age, mental ability, sex or other similar characteristics.

    Odell, C. W., Educational Measurement in the High School, p. 501.

I

i. Abbreviation for class interval.

I. B. Abbreviation for index of brightness.

I. E. R. Tests. A point scale for the measurement of intelligence. The tests were developed by the Institute of Educational Research.

    Pintner, R., Intelligence Testing, p. 209.
    Symonds, P., Measurement in Secondary Education, pp. 378-380.

I. Q. Abbreviation for intelligence quotient.

Index of Brightness (I. B.). The index of brightness is a measure of intelligence as compared with age. Thus it is in some ways similar to the intelligence quotient or coefficient of intelligence, but it is based upon a fundamentally different assumption. It was suggested by Otis in connection with his general intelligence scales and has not received extensive use in other connections. It is found by calculating the difference between an individual's score and the norm for his age and then according as this difference is plus or minus, adding it to or subtracting it from 100. Thus an index of brightness of 100 is the same as an intelligence quotient of 100, but for other values the two measures are not likely to correspond exactly or even closely.

>Freeman, F. N., Mental Tests, p. 283f.
>Otis, A. S., Statistical Method in Educational Measurements, p. 155f.

Index of Reliability. Just as the coefficient of reliability is a measure of the correlation or agreement between the scores resulting from two administrations of the same test or two duplicate forms thereof, so the index of reliability is a measure of the correlation or agreement between one of these sets of actually obtained scores and the corresponding true scores. If the coefficient of reliability is known, the index of reliability is very easily obtained since it is merely the square root of the coefficient. *See coefficient of reliability, reliable.*

>Monroe, W. S., Introduction to the Theory of Educational Measurement, p. 206f.
>Odell, C. W., Statistical Method in Education, p. 215.

Individual Differences. This expression refers to the differences between individuals, usually school pupils, in native ability or achievement, industry, attitude, interests, health, and the many other characteristics in which they may differ. The frequent occurrence of the term in recent educational and psychological literature and discussions has been due to the fact that until a relatively recent date comparatively few persons realized the number or extent of such differences.

>Brueckner, L. J., and Melby, E. O., Diagnostic and Remedial Teaching, pp. 17–48.
>Freeman, F. N., Mental Tests, p. 367f.
>Kelley, T. L., Interpretation of Educational Measurements, p. 10.
>Orleans, J. S., Measurement in Education, pp. 38, 43, 394.
>Otis, A. S., Statistical Method in Educational Measurements, p. 140.

Individual Intelligence Test. A test for measuring the mental ability and which is to be administered to only one person at a time as contrasted with group tests of intelligence. The Stanford-Binet test is an illustration. The materials of such a test are usually of such a type and used in such a manner as to make it impossible to apply them to more than one person at a time.

    Pintner, R., Intelligence Testing, pp. 135–179.

Individual Test. An individual test is one which can be administered to only one person at a time. The usual reason is that the subject's responses are oral or that the examiner must note down a rather careful description of them. Except in oral reading there are very few individual achievement tests, but in the field of intelligence testing their use is more common.

    Pintner, R., Intelligence Testing, pp. 135–179.
    Symonds, P., Measurement in Secondary Education, p. 55.

Informal Test. A test prepared by a classroom teacher is sometimes called an informal test to distinguish it from a standardized test. Such a test is generally not repeated again in the same form and is used as a classroom test only.

    Greene, H. A. and Jorgensen, A. N., Use and Interpretation of High School Tests, pp. 60–62.
    Odell, C. W., Educational Measurement in the High School, pp. 21, 41, 473.
    Ruch, G. M. and Stoddard, G. D., Tests and Measurements in High School Instruction, pp. 295–297.
    Symonds, P., Measurement in Secondary Education, pp. 5, 473, 507, 515, 531–542.

Ink-Blot Test. A test in which the person being tested examines a series of irregular figures, usually black on a white ground, and reports what objects or scenes he can imagine in the figures. (The material commonly used consists of ink-blots. Variety or speed of response is commonly the basis of scoring.) The Rorschach ink-blot test is an illustration.

Intelligence. The capacity of certain organisms to meet new situations quickly and successfully; ability to sense a problem, to make an effort to solve the problem, and to judge one's attempted solution. *See general intelligence.*

    Freeman, F. N., Mental Tests, pp. 476–491.
    Pintner, R., Intelligence Testing, pp. 45–50.

Intelligence Quotient (I. Q.). The intelligence quotient is by far the most commonly used means of comparing intelligence as measured by a general intelligence test with age. It is found by dividing an individual's mental age, derived from his score on a general intelligence test, by his chronological age. That is,

$$I.Q. = \frac{M.A.}{C.A.}.$$

In writing it the decimal point is ordinarily omitted. Thus a pupil whose mental age is the same as the average for all persons of his chronological age, has an intelligence quotient of 100. If his mental age is greater than his chronological age, his intelligence quotient is proportionately greater and if less, the I. Q. is under 100. For adults and persons in their upper teens the actual chronological age is not used as a divisor, but instead a fixed age supposed to represent the point at which the growth of intelligence ceases is employed. Sixteen has been most commonly used for this purpose though several other ages within two or three years of this have been suggested.

    Brueckner, L. J., and Melby, E. O., Diagnostic and Remedial Teaching, p. 99.
    Freeman, F. N., Mental Tests, pp. 98, 276f.
    Pintner, R., Intelligence Testing, p. 445.

Intelligence Scale. A series of scaled mental tests, by which the degree of intelligence, or mental development, of an individual may be determined. (e. g., the Binet-Simon Scale.)

Intelligence Test. Synonymous with general intelligence test.

Interval (i). Synonymous with class interval.

Introversion-Extroversion Test. A test designed to measure the degree to which a person tends, in his attitudes and behavior, toward the reflective, self-centered type, or the energetic, externally-minded type.

Interview. A conference between two persons. An interview must be felt necessary by the student or the act of counseling will not have the desired end.

    Jones, A. J., Principles of Guidance, pp. 277-278.

Inventory Test. An inventory test is one used to determine the ability and knowledge of pupils in a certain field of subject matter at the beginning of a period of instruction. An inventory test, therefore, usually covers a particular field of subject matter rather thoroughly. It is more or less synonymous with diagnostic test, but not absolutely so.

Orleans, J. S., Measurement in Education, pp. 310, 316.

Inverse Correlation. Synonymous with negative correlation.

Irregular Test. An irregular test is one in which the exercises vary in difficulty and are not arranged in order of increasing or decreasing difficulty. Most tests which contain exercises not selected on the basis of difficulty are of this sort. In scoring, irregular tests are usually treated as uniform; that is, each item or exercise counts the same amount. Unless the irregularities are extreme, this procedure is unlikely to introduce serious errors in the pupils' scores.

Monroe, W. S., Introduction to the Theory of Educational Measurement, pp. 62, 75, 108.

Item. An item is the smallest unit of test construction. Sometimes an item is the same as an exercise; sometimes there are a number of items in a single exercise. Each statement in a true-false test, each blank to be filled in a completion test, each one of several suggested answers in a multiple-choice test, is an item.

Greene, H. A., and Jorgensen, A. N., Use and Interpretation of High School Tests, p. 70.
Odell, C. W., Educational Measurement in the High School, p. 75.

Item Analysis. Any one of several methods used in test construction to determine whether a given question or task discriminates between individuals of different degrees of ability.

J

Job Analysis. An act of analyzing a job as to the various kinds of skills, abilities, habits or attitudes which an individual finds that job requires.

Jones, A. J., Principles of Guidance, pp. 9, 161, 263, 273.

K

Kent-Rosanoff Test. A free association test consisting of a list of 100 stimulus words. This test was devised by A. J. Rosanoff in 1910. It is used for clinical purposes in making a mental diagnosis.

L

Law of the Single Variable. The law of the single variable is that in making educational measurements, all of the factors which control or affect pupils' performances should be held constant save one, and this one measured. For example, if one wishes to measure rate of reading, such other factors as difficulty of the material read, quality or accuracy of reading, and all the conditions under which the test is given should be controlled or made uniform. A somewhat broader interpretation sometimes given the law of the single variable is that it merely demands the explicit recognition and separate description of the different dimensions, ordinarily three, of pupil performance. Since in many cases it is practically impossible to insure that all the variables except one are constant, this latter interpretation is the one most generally given. *See performance, variable.*

> Monroe, W. S., Introduction to the Theory of Educational Measurement, p. 87f.

Lower Quartile (Q_1). Synonymous with first quartile.

M

M. Abbreviation for mean.

M. A. Abbreviation for mental age.

M. D. Abbreviation for mean deviation.

Mg. Sometimes used as abbreviation for geometric mean.

M. I. Abbreviation for mental index.

Mental Measurement. The quantitative evaluation of a person's native abilities and tendencies. The term is often used as being synonymous to mental testing but is generally somewhat more inclusive.

Mark. The term mark is applied to ratings given pupils in terms of per cents, letters, or other symbols. Thus 75 per cent, 80 per cent, A, C, and so on, when used for this purpose are best called marks. By so doing the term grade is restricted to its general use to indicate stage of advancement within a school, such as first grade, fourth grade, and so forth, and thus confusion is avoided.

>McCall, W. A., How to Measure in Education, pp. 57–63, 154, 155.
>Odell, C. W., Educational Measurement in the High School, p. 458.
>Pressey, S. L., and Cole, L., Introduction to the Use of Standard Tests, pp. 15, 58, 218.
>Ruch, G. M, .and Stoddard, G. D., Tests and Measurements in High School Instruction, pp. 254–265.
>Symonds, P., Measurement in Secondary Education, p. 480f.

Matching Test. This form of test question is one of the forms used in the new-type examination and standardized tests. In such a test there are two columns of words or other expressions and the pupils are asked to match those in one column with those in the other. For example, the first column may consist of a list of books, the second of authors.

>Odell, C. W., Educational Measurement in the High School, p. 492.
>Orleans, J. S., Measurement in Education, pp. 57, 450.

Md. Most common abbreviation for median.

Md. D. Abbreviation for median deviation.

Mean (M). The mean is the same measure that is usually called the average or the arithmetic average. It is found by dividing the sum of a number of scores or measures by their number. That is to say,

$$M_x = \frac{\sum x}{N}.$$

The term mean rather than average is preferable in this connection so that the latter can be saved for a more inclusive use and thus confusion avoided. *See average.*

>Odell, C. W., Statistical Method in Education, pp. 67, 97–98.
>Otis, A. S., Statistical Method in Educational Measurements, pp. 6f., 17f., 37f.

Mean Deviation (M. D.). As is implied, this is the mean or average of the deviations of a set of measures from a given point. Theoretically this point may be any measure of central tendency— that is, any average, using the term in its broad sense; but as a matter of practice the mean deviation is always found around either the mean or the median.

> Odell, C. W., Statistical Method in Education, pp. 119, 132, 136, 184.
> Otis, A. S., Statistical Method in Educational Measurements, pp. 88, 90, 93.

Measure. An evaluation obtained by measurement; a value or score.

Measurement. The comparison of something with a standard amount or unit in order to discover how many times the standard amount is contained in the original.

Mechanical Intelligence. A general capacity on the part of an individual for dealing with mechanisms.

> Pintner, R., Intelligence Testing, pp. 55–62.

Med. An abbreviation for median.

Median (Md. or Med.). The median is that point on the scale which divides the total number of measures or cases into two equal groups. Thus if there are 90 cases, the median is a point such that 45 of the cases lie at or below it and 45 at or above it. Sometimes a distinction is made between a grouped distribution or frequency table and a simple or ungrouped series in that the term median is used in connection with the former and mid-score or mid-measure with the latter. Although such a distinction seems desirable it is not common, but the term median is generally used to include both cases.

> Greene, H. A., and Jorgensen, A. N., Use and Interpretation of High School Tests, pp. 167, 168, 170.
> Odell, C. W., Educational Measurement in the High School, pp. 30, 557, 598.
> Odell, C. W., Statistical Method in Education, pp. 77, 98.
> Orleans, J. S., Measurement in Education, p. 408.
> Otis, A. S., Statistical Method in Educational Measurements, pp. 11f, 43f.
> Pressey, S. L., and Cole, L., Introduction to the Use of Standard Tests, pp. 47, 227.

Median Deviation (Md. D.). The median deviation is merely the median of the deviations about a given point. The point taken for this purpose is almost always the mean. Fifty per cent of the scores or measures in a normal distribution lie not more than one median deviation from the mean and the other 50 per cent not less than this distance from it. Although the median deviation could be found by tabulating the actual deviations and determining their median, this method is rarely, if ever, used. Instead the standard deviation is computed and multiplied by .6745 to determine the median deviation. This relationship holds exactly only in the case of a normal distribution, but for distributions not extremely different from the normal it is accurate enough for most purposes. The median deviation is often miscalled the probable error, a term which is correctly applied only when it is used in connection with errors. *See deviation, probable error.*

Odell, C. W., Statistical Method in Education, pp. 58, 132, 137, 439.
Otis, A. S., Statistical Method in Educational Measurements, pp. 88, 93, 94, 99, 224, 294.

Mental Age (M. A.). A pupil's score on a general intelligence test expressed in terms of age is called his mental age. To say that a pupil has a mental age of a certain amount—for example, ten years and six months—means that his intelligence test score is the average or median score made by an unselected or random group of pupils ten years and six months of age chronologically.

Freeman, F. N., Mental Tests, p. 84.
Odell, C. W., Educational Measurement in the High School, pp. 32, 443.
Pintner, R., Intelligence Testing, pp. 28, 114–116, 118, 155–156.

Mental Index (M. I.). Mental index is one of the measures of native ability which has been suggested but has received little use. It is determined according to a scale based upon an assumption of normal distribution of ability and such that the lowest possible value is zero, the average or normal value, 50, and the highest possible value, 100. The mental index is, therefore, intended to perform the same function as the intelligence of an individual with the average intelligence of individuals of his age. The method of computing it, however, is distinctly different from that for the intelligence quotient and therefore these measures cannot be compared directly.

Mental Ratio. Synonymous with I. Q.

Mental Test. *See intelligence test.*

Mid-Measure. Synonymous with mid-score.

Mid-Score. The mid-score may be defined as the middle measure when a series of measures or scores is arranged in order of size. If there is an odd number of cases it is always an actual measure, but if the number is even the average of the two mid-most measures is taken.

>Odell, C. W., Statistical Method in Education, pp. 77, 86, 98.
>Otis, A. S., Statistical Method in Educational Measurements, p. 11.

Miniature Test. This type of test, which is rarely used except in connection with vocational prognosis, involves a small-scale reproduction of the actual performances in which ability is to be tested. A well-known example of the miniature test was constructed by Munsterberg to predict the ability of motormen. He constructed in the laboratory a chart which represented a street with the various factors and difficulties which must be dealt with in operating a street-car represented upon it. The prospective motormen were required to respond to this situation. Both speed and accuracy were counted in the scoring of the test.

>Freeman, F. N., Mental Tests, p. 412.
>McCall, W. A., How to Measure in Education, p. 197.

Mixed Relations Test. Synonymous with analogies test.

Mode (Z). The mode of a distribution is that point on the scale at which there are more measures than are to be found at any other point. Thus in a sense the mode may be said to be the typical value or case. In a grouped distribution or frequency table the true mode cannot be determined by inspection but requires rather difficult computation. In such cases it is frequently the practice not to state the mode as a definite point but merely to say that it lies within the interval which contains the greatest frequency. Sometimes one of two or three fairly easy formulae which give approximation to the true mode is employed. The most commonly used of these is that the mode equals three times the median less twice the mean, or $Z = 3Md. - 2M$. Occasionally the term mode is used in a broader sense to apply to any point on the scale at which the frequency is greater than are the frequencies immediately above and below that point. In this sense a distribution or curve may have two or more modes. In such cases the one at which the frequency is greatest is called the major mode.

>Odell, C. W., Statistical Method in Education, pp. 87, 98.
>Otis, A. S., Statistical Method in Educational Measurements, pp. 18, 19.

M-Scale. The M-scale is similar to the much better known T-scale, except that it is based upon the ability of a particular group of children and can be used only with that group whereas the T-scale is based upon the ability of twelve-year-old children in general. Both are based upon the assumption of normal distribution of ability and provide scales in terms of which the difficulty of exercises and pupils' scores may be expressed. *See T-scale.*

    McCall, W. A., How to Measure in Education, pp. 272–292.
    Odell, C. W., Educational Measurement in the High School, p. 447.

M-Score. A score given according to the M-scale.

Multi-Modal. A frequency distribution or curve is said to be multi-modal when it includes two or more points at each of which the frequencies are greater than those next to them in each case. In other words, a distribution or curve having more than one mode in the broader sense of the word is called multi-modal. *See mode.*

    Odell, C. W., Statistical Method in Education, p. 90.

Multimodal Theory of Intelligence. "Intelligence is a pattern of an indefinite number of specific capacities." (Thorndike.) *See factor theory.*

Multiple-Answer Test. A multiple-answer test is composed of exercises which require pupils to select one or more correct answers out of a group of several given in the exercises. There are many possible forms and varieties of such exercises.

    Greene, H. A., and Jorgensen, A. N., Use and Interpretation of High School Tests, pp. 79, 81–82.
    Odell, C. W., Educational Measurement in the High School, p. 486.
    Orleans, J. S., Measurement in Education, pp. 56, 440.
    Ruch, G. M., and Stoddard, G. D., Tests and Measurement in High School Instruction, pp. 267f., 273f.

Multiple-Choice Test. Synonymous with multiple-answer test.

Multiple Correlation. Multiple correlation is the correlation of one variable with two or more other variables in combination. It is almost always expressed in terms of a coefficient of correlation which is computed from the ordinary or product-moment coefficients of correlation between the various pairs of variables involved. *See coefficient of multiple correlation, correlation.*

    Odell, C. W., Statistical Method in Education, p. 283.
    Otis, A. S., Statistical Method in Educational Measurements, p. 238f.

N

N. This letter is used as the abbreviation for the total number of cases in a frequency table. In cases in which a whole group and a sub-group are dealt with, N is commonly used for the entire group and n for the sub-group.

Negative Correlation. Correlation or relationship which is such that the larger values of one variable or series of facts tend to be associated with the smaller values of the other and vice versa, is called negative. *See correlation, positive correlation.*

    Odell, C. W., Statistical Method in Education, p. 144.
    Otis, A. S., Statistical Method in Educational Measurements, pp. 200–201.

New Examination. This term has been very commonly employed to include those types of tests or exercises which call for very brief pupil responses in the form of checks, underlyings, single words, and so forth, and which permit objective or near-objective scoring. Among the most common types of exercises included under this heading are multiple-answer, true-false, completion, matching, recall, and analogies. These examinations are also spoken of as new-type examinations.

    Odell, C. W., Educational Measurement in the High School, pp. 21, 41, 473.
    Ruch, G. M., and Stoddard, G. D., Tests and Measurements in High School Instruction, pp. 270–272.
    Symonds, P., Measurement in Secondary Education, pp. 473, 515, 531–532.
    Greene, H. A., and Jorgensen, A. N., Use and Interpretation of High School Tests, p. 59.

New-Type Examination. Synonymous with new examination.

New-Type Test. Synonymous with new-type examination.

Non-Language Test. Synonymous with non-verbal test.

Non-Verbal Test. Strictly speaking, a non-verbal test is one in which there is no use of words either by the examiner in giving the test or by the subjects in responding to it. Ordinarily, however, the term is more broadly applied to include all tests to which the subjects respond without using language and in which no written directions are employed, regardless of whether or not oral directions are given by the examiner. Such tests are commonly used in testing small children, illiterates, and foreigners.

 Freeman, F. N., Mental Tests, pp. 167f., 261f.
 Pintner, R., Intelligence Testing, p. 215.

Norm. A norm for a test is a statement of the actual achievement of pupils of the given age or other homogeneous group for which the norm is being determined. Therefore, a norm is merely a statement of present achievement and not of what achievement should be. It has, however, frequently been used in the latter sense. It is decidedly preferable not to do so but to use the word standard instead whenever reference is made to what pupils should do. In most cases the average or median achievement of a group is taken as the norm, but sometimes other points, such as quartiles or percentiles, are used. Most norms are general norms; that is, they are based upon the scores from a fairly large number of pupils who are more or less widely scattered over the country. In addition to these, however, local norms for particular states, cities, or even buildings are sometimes used.

 Brueckner, L. J., and Melby, E. O., Diagnostic and Remedial Teaching, p. 86.
 Monroe, W. S., Introduction to the Theory of Educational Measurement, p. 161f.
 Orleans, J. S., Measurement in Education, pp. 33, 128.
 Pressey, S. L., and Cole, L., Introduction to the Use of Standard Tests, pp. 16, 65.
 Ruch, G. M., and Stoddard, G. D., Tests and Measurements in High School Instruction, pp. 60f., 343f.
 Symonds, P., Measurement in Secondary Education, pp. 254f., 265f.

Normal Distribution. Synonymous with normal frequency distribution.

Normal Frequency Curve. *See normal frequency distribution.*

Normal Frequency Distribution. Normal frequency distribution is one which when graphed forms the familiar bell-shaped, symmetrical curve known as the normal frequency curve, the curve of error, the normal probability curve, or the Gaussian curve. This curve is high in the center, decreases in height rather rapidly near the center, and then more slowly near the extremes. It never actually touches the baseline. The normal distribution occurs more often than any other in educational and other biological data as well as in the operation of the laws of chance when the chances are equal.

> Odell, C. W., Statistical Method in Education, pp. 53, 132, 378, 439.

Normal Probability Curve. Synonymous with normal frequency curve.

O

Objective. A measuring instrument is said to be objective when different persons using it to measure the same thing secure the same results. In other words, a test is objective when there is no doubt in the opinions of competent scorers as to what the correct answers are and when all possible answers must be either definitely right or wrong.

> Monroe, W. S., Introduction to the Theory of Educational Measurement, pp. 26f., 196.
> Ruch, G. M., and Stoddard, G. D., Tests and Measurements in High School Instruction, p. 58f.

Objective Test. Sometimes the term objective test is used synonymously with new examination, because most of the forms included under that term possess relatively high objectivity. On other occasions it is employed to refer to any test, whether standardized or not, which permits no reasonable doubt as to the correctness or incorrectness of all possible answers. *See objective, new examinations.*

> Brueckner, L. J., and Melby, E. O., Diagnostic and Remedial Teaching, pp. 64, 144, 147, 149, 157.

Objectivity. *See objective.*

Ogive. The ogive or cumulative frequency curve is the curve which represents a cumulative frequency table or distribution. The ogive is ordinarily drawn as a smooth curve, though rarely the polygon or histogram form is used. In connection with an ogive it is very common to have two vertical scales. In such cases one of these indicates the actual frequencies and the other the percentile points.

> Odell, C. W., Statistical Method in Education, p. 48.
> Otis, A. S., Statistical Method in Educational Measurements, pp. 32f., 43f., 77f.

Omnibus Test. An omnibus test is one in which various kinds of tasks or exercises are mixed together in either regular or irregular order instead of being grouped in sub-tests, each of which contains exercises of only a single type. Thus there may be an analogies exercise, an example in arithmetic, a statement to be marked true or false, a multiple-answer exercise, a second analogies exercise, a completion statement, and so on. When the term omnibus test is applied in the field of school achievement it is commonly understood that the test covers several different fields of subject matter. This is, however, not necessarily implied by the name.

Symonds, P., Measurement in Secondary Education, pp. 76, 284, 378.

Opposites Test. This form of test is one of the new examination types and is also used in some standardized tests, especially those of intelligence and vocabulary. It consists of a list of terms for each of which an opposite is to be given. Sometimes, but rarely, the term is used as synonymous with the *same or opposites test*. The pupil may need to supply the opposite word himself, but more frequently he selects one from a list of five as in a multiple choice form of question. Sometimes opposites are included in the free association test materials.

Overlapping. This term is employed to describe the relative positions of two distributions on the same scale of measurement. Overlapping is usually measured and stated in terms of the proportion or per cent of one distribution which extends beyond the median or occasionally some other point of the other distribution with which it is being compared.

Odell, C. W., Statistical Method in Education, p. 401.
Otis, A. S., Statistical Method in Educational Measurements, pp. 3, 15, 87.

P

P. One of the two common abbreviations for percentile.

P. E. The abbreviation for probable error. A subscript is frequently employed to indicate the situation or derived measure to which the probable error refers. Thus the subscript $M.$ is used to denote the probable error of the mean, $Md.$ that of the median, r that of the coefficient of correlation, and so on.

Odell, C. W., Statistical Method in Education, pp. 132, 326.
Otis, A. S., Statistical Method in Educational Measurements, pp. 89, 249.

P. E.$_{est.}$ Abbreviation for probable error of estimate.

P. E.$_{meas.}$ Abbreviation for probable error of measurement.

Pantomime Test. A pantomime test is the same as a non-verbal test in the narrowest sense of the term. It is a test in which no written or spoken language is used to communicate to the subjects what they are to do, but pantomime or illustrative actions by the examiner are employed for this purpose. The chief use of such tests is in measuring the abilities of persons who are unable to understand the language spoken by the examiner.

Parallel Group. In the two-group or equivalent-group method of experimentation the groups concerned are sometimes spoken of as parallel groups. *See equivalent group method.*

Part. Most frequently this term is used to apply to a portion of a test or a test of a series which is intended for use in one or more grades, the other portions or tests each being intended for use in other grades or combinations thereof. Thus Part 1 of a test may be for use in Grades III and IV, Part 2 in Grades V and VI, and Part 3 in Grades VII and VIII. Occasionally the term part is used in some other sense to signify a portion of a test or a test of a series that covers different content or is in different form from the other portion thereof.

Partial Correlation. Partial correlation is a method of correlation involving three or more variables in which that portion of the correlation between two of them which is not due to nor common with the others included, is determined. In other words, the influence of all the variables except two is held constant or eliminated and the correlation between those two determined. Partial correlation is practically always expressed in terms of the coefficient of partial correlation, which is calculated from ordinary product-moment coefficients of correlation. *See coefficient of partial correlation, correlation.*

 Odell, C. W., Statistical Method in Education, p. 263.
 Otis, A. S., Statistical Method in Educational Measurements, pp. 230, 233.

Per. Abbreviation for percentile.

Percentile (Per. or P.). The percentiles are the points which divide the total number of cases contained in a frequency distribution into 100 equal parts; that is, into 100 parts each of which contains the same number of cases. The percentile is the smallest unit of division ordinarily employed in connection with frequency distributions.

Kelley, T. L., Interpretation of Educational Measurements, p. 185f.
Odell, C. W., Statistical Method in Education, pp. 50, 109.
Otis, A. S., Statistical Method in Educational Measurements, pp. 26, 95, 118.

Percentile Curve. Synonymous with ogive.

Percentile Norm. Although the standard method of stating norms is in terms of the median, which is the same as the fiftieth percentile, this is not infrequently supplemented by a statement of other points in the distribution. Sometimes the scores corresponding to the tenth, twentieth, and every successive tenth percentile are given and sometimes those at other percentile points. The value of such norms is that one can compare not merely the median or average achievement of a class with them, but also the achievement of pupils at any point in the distribution.

Orleans, J. S., Measurement in Education, pp. 62, 136.
Ruch, G. M., and Stoddard, G. D., Tests and Measurements in High School Instruction, p. 347f.

Percentile Rank. Synonymous with percentile score.

Percentile Score. A percentile score is a statement of a pupil's score in terms of his relative or percentile position in the distribution of scores of the whole group to which he belongs. A percentile score of a given amount, as, for example, 66, means that his score is equal to or better than the scores of the given per cent, in this case 66, of the pupils in the group. For the comparison of scores made by the same pupil on different tests or by different pupils, percentile scores are often very useful.

Greene, H. A., and Jorgensen, A. N., Use and Interpretation of High School Tests, pp. 204–206.
Monroe, W. S., Introduction to the Theory of Educational Measurement, p. 154f.
Otis, A. S., Statistical Method in Educational Measurements, pp. 26f., 95f, 118f.

Performance. A pupil's performance is what he does. On group tests his performance is always or practically always written and the same is true for some individual tests. To be useful for testing purposes it must be such that a competent observer or scorer can easily observe it. Performance, what a pupil does, is to be distinguished from ability or capacity, what he might or is able to do.

Greene, H. A., and Jorgensen, A. N., Use and Interpretation of High School Tests, p. 210.

Performance Test or Scale. A performance test or scale is composed of exercises which require the subject to react to problems presented in the form of concrete objects rather than of words, instructions being either verbal or pantomime. Thus a performance test is a variety of non-verbal test. Indeed, the two terms are sometimes used interchangeably, but in its broader sense the non-verbal test is more inclusive than the performance test.

Freeman, F. N., Mental Tests, p. 158f.
Pintner, R., Intelligence Testing, pp. 41, 159–164.

Personal Equation. It has been discovered that in measurements involving observation there tend to be constant errors present in the cases of all series of observations and that the amounts of these errors differ with different observers. This difference in the amount of error has been called the personal equation. *See subjective.*

Freeman, F. N., Mental Tests, p. 32f.

Personality. All of an individual's characteristics both native and acquired.

Jones, A. J., Principles of Guidance, pp. 55–56.

Point Scale. In a broad sense a point scale may be said to be any scale which makes use of scores computed in terms of points. The expression has, however, been generally limited to apply to general intelligence scales which are scored in terms of points as contrasted with those scored in terms of months or years of mental age. Ordinarily age norms are given in connection with such scales so that any obtained point score may be transmuted into a corresponding mental age.

Freeman, F. N., Mental Tests, p. 131f.
Pintner, R., Intelligence Testing, pp. 146–149, 173.

Point Score. A point score is the score yielded directly by a test. It may be in terms of exercises done correctly, exercises attempted, level of difficulty reached, and so forth. It is only by chance that point scores upon two or more different tests have the same meaning with regard to the amount of achievement or ability which they represent or indicate. In many cases provision is made for turning point scores into derived scores of various sorts. *See derived score.*

Freeman, F. N., Mental Tests, p. 265.
Monroe, W. S., Introduction to the Theory of Educational Measurement, p. 292.

Positive Correlation. The correlation or relationship between two variables or sets of paired measures is called positive when there is a tendency for large measures in one series to be associated with large measures in the other, and vice versa. *See correlation, negative correlation.*

    Greene, H. A., and Jorgensen, J. N., Use and Interpretation of High School Tests, pp. 189–190.
    McCall, W. A., How to Measure in Education, pp. 389, 396.
    Odell, C. W., Statistical Method in Education, pp. 66, 143.
    Otis, A. S., Statistical Method in Educational Measurements, p. 4.

Power Test. A scaled test—that is, a test arranged in order of increasing difficulty of exercises which yields only a difficulty score—is called a power test. Such an instrument measures the power or ability of pupils to do increasingly difficult exercises of the same kind, hence the name. Sometimes the term is used as entirely synonymous with scaled test regardless of the method of scoring.

    Greene, H. A., and Jorgensen, J. N., Use and Interpretation of High School Tests, p. 15, 25.
    Kelley, T. L., Interpretation of Educational Measurements, p. 31.
    Monroe, W. S., Introduction to the Theory of Educational Measurement, p. 63.
    Orleans, J. S., Measurement in Education, p. 108.
    Symonds, P., Measurement in Secondary Education, pp. 117, 120.

Practice Effect. Practice effect refers to the increase of the scores of one trial over those yielded by a preceding trial of the same test when there has been no coaching between the two administrations of the test. The term is commonly used to refer to the average increase of the scores of a group of pupils, but sometimes in connection with the increase between the scores of an individual pupil. Through becoming acquainted with testing procedure and the nature of the exercises pupils tend to make higher scores on the second trial than on the first, still higher on the third, than on the second, and so on. In general, however, the increase from the first trial to the second is much greater than that from the second to the third. This tendency continues, until after perhaps the fourth or fifth trial there is often very little or no further increase.

    Monroe, W. S., Introduction to the Theory of Educational Measurement, p. 167f.
    Otis, A. S., Statistical Method in Educational Measurements, p. 264f.
    Pintner, R., Intelligence Testing, p. 93.
    Symonds, P., Measurement in Secondary Education, pp. 273–274.

Practice Test. This expression is used in two senses. In one it is synonymous with preliminary test or fore-exercise. In the other it refers to a test which has as its function giving pupils practice in the abilities covered rather than measuring their achievements thereon. Such practice tests are most common in arithmetic, but also exist in algebra, language, and other subjects. Usually a rather large number of them are included in one series. Such practice tests or lessons are used in several prognostic tests.

    Brueckner, L. J., and Melby, E. O., Diagnostic and Remedial Teaching, pp. 187, 426, 486.
    Odell, C. W., Educational Measurement in the High School, p. 24.

Preliminary Test. Synonymous with fore-exercise.

Pre-Test. A practice test or a test given to establish an ability before further testing.

Principle. Principles include laws, rules, truths and certain other important statements. In other words, a principle may be thought of as a statement or criterion, usually generalized, by which the truth or validity of a proposed plan, a suggested theory, or a tentative conclusion may be tested.

Probability. The likeliness of the occurrence of an event. It is expressed as a ratio between the number of ways in which an event may occur and the number of ways in which alternate events may occur.

Probability Curve. Synonymous with normal frequency curve.

Probable Error (P. E.). The term probable error should be limited in use to apply to the median deviation when used as a measure of the errors present in data of any sort. It is also frequently but improperly used as completely synonymous with median deviation. In either usage half of the deviations or errors in a normal distribution are less than the probable error and the other half are greater. In other words, the chances are even or one to one that any particular error is greater or less than the probable error. In educational work the probable error is the most commonly used measure of errors. It is ordinarily assumed that errors form a normal distribution and, therefore, that the same interpretation of the probable error applies in all cases. Usually the approximation to a normal distribution is close enough to justify this assumption.

A subscript is frequently employed with the abbreviation for the probable error to indicate the measure to which it belongs. Thus $P.\ E._M$ refers to the probable error of the mean, $P.\ E._Q$ to that of the quartile deviation, and so forth. *See median deviation.*
    Odell, C. W., Statistical Method in Education, pp. 132, 326.
    Otis, A. S., Statistical Method in Educational Measurements, pp. 89, 248, 249, 252.
    Monroe, W. S., Introduction to the Theory of Educational Measurement, p. 327.

Probable Error of Estimate (P. E.$_{est}$). This is merely the probable error applied to errors of estimate.

$$P.\ E._{est.}\ .6745\ \sigma\ \sqrt{1 - r^2}\ .$$

    Monroe, W. S., Introduction to the Theory of Educational Measurement, p. 348f.
    Odell, C. W., Statistical Method in Education, p. 363.

Probable Error of Measurement (P. E.$_{meas}$). This refers to the use of the probable error in connection with errors of measurement. It is derived from the probable error of estimate. There are several formulae of which the most common is

$$P.\ E._{meas.} = .6745\ \sigma\ \sqrt{1 - r}\ .$$

    Kelley, T. L., Interpretation of Educational Measurements, p. 171f.
    Monroe, W. S., Introduction to the Theory of Educational Measurement, pp. 207f., 354.
    Odell, C. W., Statistical Method in Education, p. 366.

Problem. In educational and psychological research the term problem is used to designate the question or questions to which answers are sought. It may be expressed by a declarative statement of the purpose of the investigation as a hypothesis to be proved or may be definitely in question form.

Product-Moment Correlation. This name is given to the usual method of computing the coefficient of correlation, a method devised by Karl Pearson. For a small number of cases, perhaps less than 25 or 30, the data are usually arranged in two columns, the corresponding entries in which constitute a pair of measures, whereas for larger numbers of cases a correlation or double entry table is almost always used. The formula used in product-moment correlation compares the deviations of the corresponding pairs of measures from their means with the standard deviations of the two distributions and thus yields the coefficient of correlation. Its general form is

$$r = \frac{\sum xy}{\sqrt{\sum x^2 \cdot \sum y^2}} \quad \text{or} \quad r = \frac{\sum xy}{N\sigma_x \cdot \sigma_y}.$$

See coefficient of correlation, correlation.

>Odell, C. W., Statistical Method in Education, p. 320.
>Otis, A. S., Statistical Method in Educational Measurements, pp. 186, 189.

Profile Chart. A curve uniting the points representing a pupil's scores or relative position in each of several types of performance. An educational profile compares the pupil's achievements in several school subjects; a psychograph displays his standings in a number of traits.

>Kelley, T. L., Interpretation of Educational Measurements, p. 131.

Prognosis. The prediction of a student's probable success in a specific subject-matter field or in general.

>Odell, C. W., Educational Measurement in the High School, pp. 47, 520.
>Symonds, P., Measurement in Secondary Education, pp. 7, 393, 436.

Prognostic Test. A test which has for its function the prediction or prognosis of a pupil's status. Such a prediction is based upon the pupil's performance at the present. All, or practically all, tests have prognostic value, but those which have been devised especially for this purpose are in general more valid. The tests used for prognostic purposes may be intelligence tests, achievement tests, or tests which strictly speaking belong under neither of these classifications. Such tests are called aptitude tests.

>Greene, H. A., and Jorgensen, A. N., Use and Interpretation of High School Tests, pp. 21, 402–405, 453–454.
>Monroe, W. S., Introduction to the Theory of Educational Measurements, p. 223.
>Monroe, W. S., DeVoss, J. C., and Kelly, F. J., Educational Tests and Measurements, pp. 299, 307, 321.
>Odell, C. W., Educational Measurement in the High School, pp. 23, 522.
>Orleans, J. S., Measurement in Education, pp. 66, 151.
>Ruch, G. M., and Stoddard, G. D., Tests and Measurements in High School Instruction, p. 39f.
>Symonds, P., Measurement in Secondary Education, p. 363f.

Psychograph. A chart used to indicate an individual's measure or standing in fundamental traits.

>Freeman, F. N., Mental Tests, p. 119.

Psychometric. The term psychometric refers to the measurement of mentality in its broadest sense; that is, including general intelligence, ability in specific subjects, emotional qualities, and so forth.

Q

Q. Abbreviation for quartile deviation.

Q_1. Abbreviation for first or lower quartile.

Q_2 Abbreviation for second quartile.

Q_3. Abbreviation for third or upper quartile.

Quality. One of three dimensions concerned in measuring pupils' performances. Often this characteristic is described in terms of per cent of exercises done correctly. In such cases quality is synonymous with accuracy. Certain types of performances, such as handwriting and drawing, cannot be classified as either right or wrong. In such instances, quality may be defined as merit and is described in terms of a quality scale with which the specimens produced by the pupils are compared or evaluated. *See accuracy.*

> Greene, H. A., and Jorgensen, A. N., Use and Interpretation of High School Tests, p. 26.
> Monroe, W. S., Introduction to the Theory of Educational Measurement, p. 108f.
> Odell, C. W., Educational Measurement in the High School, p. 19.
> Pressey, S. L., and Cole, L., Introduction to the Use of Standard Tests, p. 98.

Quality Scale. A scale composed of a set of samples or specimens arranged in order of merit. Pupils' performances are compared with the specimens or steps on such a scale and rated by determining the ones which they most resemble. Such scales are used in cases in which pupil performances cannot be rated as definitely right or wrong. Handwriting, English composition, and drawing are subjects in which quality scales are most widely used.

> Brueckner, L. J., and Melby, E. O., Diagnostic and Remedial Teaching, p. 67.
> Greene, H. A., and Jorgensen, A. N., Use and Interpretation of High School Tests, p. 26.
> Monroe, W. S., Introduction to the Theory of Educational Measurement, p. 108f.
> Odell, C. W., Educational Measurement in the High School, p. 25.

Quantitative Method (or Methods). Synonymous with statistical method (or methods).

Quartile (Q with subscript 1, 2, or 3). The quartiles are the points which divide the total number of cases in a frequency distribution into four equal parts; that is, into four parts each of which contains the same number of cases. Thus one-fourth of all the cases lie at or below the first quartile and three-fourths at or above it. The term quartile is also sometimes applied to one of the four divisions formed by the points just mentioned. *See first quartile, second quartile, third quartile.*

    Odell, C. W., Statistical Method in Education, p. 105.
    Otis, A. S., Statistical Method in Educational Measurements, p. 33.

Quartile deviation. *See deviation quartile.*

Questionnaire. The questionnaire consists of a more or less formal list of questions, copies of which are sent to a number of persons with the request that they fill in the answers and return. They vary with reference to the types of questions asked. Some call for facts in possession of the recipient or easily obtainable by him. Others require him to collect information and perhaps even to make calculations. Still a third type consists of questions asking for expressions of opinion. Questionnaires are least objectionable when they are of the first sort; that is, when they call for simple facts in the possession of the recipient. The questionnaire method has been very much abused. When expressions of opinion are sought, those to whom it is sent should be competent.

Quintile. A name applied to a portion of a distribution when that distribution has been divided into five equal divisions.

    Odell, C. W., Statistical Methods in Education, p. 113.

Quotient Score. A quotient score is a score which expresses a pupil's performance in comparison with his supposed ability to perform, ordinarily measured by either his general intelligence or his age. *See achievement quotient, educational quotient, ratio score.*

    Freeman, F. N., Mental Tests, p. 285f.

R

r. This is the very commonly used abbreviation for the ordinary or product-moment coefficient of correlation. It is also used for the coefficient of partial correlation, in which case it is practically always followed by two subscripts, which indicate the two variables correlated, then a dot and other subscripts, which indicate the variables eliminated or held constant, thus:

$$r_{12 \cdot 34 \ldots n}.$$

Odell, C. W., Statistical Method in Education, pp. 186, 189.
Otis, A. S., Statistical Method in Educational Measurements, p. 320.

R. This symbol is the abbreviation for two different expressions or measures used in connection with correlation. One is the coefficient of multiple correlation. When thus used R is followed by subscripts all but the first of which are either enclosed in parenthesis or follow a dot, thus: $R_{1(23 \ldots n)}$, or $R_{1 \cdot 23 \ldots n}$. The first subscript in this notation denotes the one variable which is correlated with the others in combination and of course the subscripts within the parenthesis or after the dot indicate those variables which form the combination. In its other usage R is the abbreviation for one of the coefficients of rank correlation rather commonly used. In this sense it rarely has a subscript.

Otis, A. S., Statistical Method in Educational Measurements, pp. 210, 295.

Random Error. Synonymous with variable error.

Random Sample. A sample is said to be random when it has been selected from the total population or group which it is to represent without any bias entering into its selection. *See error of sampling, sampling.*

Range. The range of a series of scores or other measures is the distance from the lowest to the highest measure. Thus the range of a group of percentile marks of which the lowest is 42 per cent and the highest 85 per cent, is 43.

Odell, C. W., Statistical Method in Education, pp. 116, 136.
Otis, A. S., Statistical Method in Educational Measurements, p. 85.

Range Scale. Test series designed to measure primarily the number and variety of tasks in which the testee has ability.

Pintner, R., Intelligence Testing, pp. 53-54.

Rank Correlation. In instances wherein comparatively small groups of individuals, usually not over 25 or 30, are concerned, it is very common to determine relationship by computing rank correlation rather than product-moment correlation. In so doing the ranks of the various individuals concerned are dealt with rather than their exact scores. The chief reason why rank correlation is used is that for such small numbers its computation is decidedly easier. When the number of cases becomes large, however, this is no longer true. There are two common methods of computing rank correlation, neither of which is quite as reliable as product-moment correlation, although the difference is not great. The formula used in one method is

$$\rho = 1 - \frac{6 \sum D^2}{N(N^2 - 1)}$$

and that in the other,

$$R = 1 - \frac{6 \sum g}{N^2 - 1}.$$

The coefficients of rank correlation obtained from these formulae may be, and usually are, turned into approximate equivalents of coefficients of product-moment correlation. *See correlation.*

Kelley, T. L., Interpretation of Educational Measurements, p. 189f.
Odell, C. W., Statistical Method in Education, p. 224.
Otis, A. S., Statistical Method in Educational Measurements, p. 206f.

Rank Order. Arrangement of a series of scores in such a way that each successive member will represent a value larger than the preceding member. It is not implied in rank order that successive differences are even approximately equal.

Otis, A. S., Statistical Method in Educational Measurements, pp. 20, 81.

Rate Score. A rate score is a measure of a pupil's speed of work. It is usually expressed in terms of the number of exercises or other units of work done within a certain time. Sometimes all those attempted are counted, sometimes only those correctly answered. A rate score may also be expressed in terms of the amount of time used by the pupil to complete a specified amount of work, but this is not so common as the preceding method.

Rate Test. A rate test is one which yields a rate score. It may yield other scores also, but must yield a rate score unaffected by the other dimensions of pupil performance.

Monroe, W. S., Introduction to the Theory of Educational Measurement, pp. 63f., 107f.
Orleans, J. S., Measurement in Education, p. 108.

Rating. An estimate of a person's qualities, by himself or another. The estimate may be qualitative or quantitative. In the latter case, the strength of the trait is judged in terms of some conventional numerical value, of a scale composed of such divisions as Very Good, Good, Average, Poor, Very Poor, or of direct comparison with other persons.

Symonds, P., Measurement in Secondary Education, pp. 333-354.

Rating Scale. *See rating and scale.*

Ratio Score. A ratio score is similar to a quotient score although the two cannot be said to be absolutely synonymous. The term ratio score is rarely used, but when employed is usually applied to the quotient obtained by dividing an achievement score expressed in terms of age by mental age. *See quotient score.*

Odell, C. W., Statistical Method in Education, p. 407.

Ratio of Correlation (eta). The ratio of correlation is the only commonly used index of curvilinear correlation or relationship. It must always be equal to or greater than the coefficient of correlation, being equal to it in case the relationship is rectilinear and being increasingly greater than it the more curvilinear the relationship is. It is always positive, ranging from $+1.00$ down to zero, and thus does not indicate whether the relationship is positive or negative. There are two ratios of correlation for each correlation table. One of these measures the curvilinear correlation of the variable shown on the horizontal scale on the one shown on the vertical scale. The other measures that of the variable shown on the vertical scale on the one represented on the horizontal scale. Using X and Y for the two variables, the formula for the ratio of X on Y is

$$\eta xy = \frac{\sqrt{\sum \frac{(\sum x)^2}{f} - cx^2}}{\sigma x}$$

and that for Y on X is

$$\eta yx = \frac{\sqrt{\sum \frac{(\sum y)^2}{f} - cy^2}}{\sigma y}$$

Odell, C. W., Statistical Method in Education, pp. 250, 324.

Raw Score. A raw score is the numerical expression or description of an individual's performance in terms of the unit used in the construction of the scale or in scoring the test. It is often spoken of as the number of questions answered correctly.

Recall Test. Synonymous with single-answer test.

Recognition Test. Synonymous with multiple-answer test.

Rectilinear Relationship. The relationship between two variables is said to be rectilinear or straight-line when a graphic representation thereof is a straight line or approaches it more nearly than any other common geometrical curve. The rectilinear relationship between two or more variables is usually summarized by the coefficient of correlation, an expression which measures this type of relationship only. For purposes of predicting or estimating scores, and so forth, the regression coefficients and equations are the measures of rectilinear relationship commonly employed.

Regression. *See coefficient of regression, regression equation.*

Regression Equation. For each correlation table showing the relationship of two variables there are two regression equations. One of these expresses the most probable or likely value of the first variable in terms of the second and the other that of the second in terms of the first. Thus these equations furnish the best means of predicting values of one variable when those of the other are known. The most convenient form of the formula for the regression of one variable, X, upon the other, Y is probably as follows:

$$X = r \frac{\sigma x}{\sigma y} y + M_x - r \frac{\sigma x}{\sigma y} My.$$

In connection with the correlation of three or more variables, partial or multiple regression equations may also be found by means of which the most probable value of one variable may be predicted in terms of all the others concerned. The regression equations are rectilinear; that is, they assume straightline relationship. *See coefficient of regression.*

Odell, C. W., Statistical Method in Education, p. 239.
Otis, A. S., Statistical Method in Educational Measurements, p. 243.

Reliability. *See reliable.*

Reliable. A test or measuring instrument is reliable to the degree to which a second application of the test yields scores equivalent to those obtained from the first application. This includes both the use of the identical test on two occasions and also of equivalent forms of the same test. In either case it will be found that some pupils make higher scores and others lower upon the second trial than on the first. Most of these differences are due to the presence of variable or accidental errors in both sets of scores. The reliability of a test is expressed in terms of a numerical coefficient or index which indicates the size of these variable errors. Constant errors do not affect reliability.

> Kelley, T. L., Interpretation of Educational Measurements, pp. 33, 35f.
> Monroe, W. S., Introduction to the Theory of Educational Measurement, p. 201f.
> Ruch, G. M., and Stoddard, G. D., Tests and Measurements in High School Instruction, pp. 51f., 355f.

Research. Research may be defined as a method of studying problems whose solutions are to be derived partly or wholly from facts. The facts dealt with in research may be statements of opinion, historical facts, those contained in records and reports, the results of tests, answers to questionnaires, experimental data of any sort, and so forth.

Rho (ρ). Abbreviation for one of the common coefficients of rank correlation.

Right-Minus-Wrong Formula. This refers to the formula commonly and preferably used in scoring alternative tests. According to it a pupil's score consists of the number of right answers minus the number of wrong answers. It is also sometimes used in connection with multiple-answer tests involving more than two possibilities. The generalized form of the formula which applies to all multiple-answer tests is:

$$\text{Score} = R - \frac{W}{N-1}.$$

In this formula R equals the number of right answers, and N the number of suggested answers in each exercise.

> Symonds, P., Measurement in Secondary Education, pp. 29, 30.

Root-Mean-Square Deviation. This term is applied to measures of deviation or variability based upon the squares of the deviations.

The only one of these measures commonly used is the standard deviation. Frequently the term is used as exactly synonymous with standard deviation but it should be followed by the qualifying phrase "from the mean" if this is done. *See standard deviation.*

Odell, C. W., Statistical Method in Education, p. 123.

Rotation Method. This is a method of arranging or organizing groups of pupils for experimentation. It involves the use of two or more groups in which the experimental factors are so rotated as to yield a more nearly equivalent basis of comparison.

S

s. Symbol for the standard deviation from some other point than the mean.

S. A. Abbreviation for subject age.

S. D. One of the abbreviations for standard deviation. See sigma (σ).

S. Q. Abbreviation for subject quotient.

S. R. Abbreviation for subject ratio.

Same or Opposites Test. This is a variety of objective test sometimes used as a form of the new examination and also in standardized tests in which a number of pairs of words or other expressions are given and the pupils are to indicate whether those in each pair mean the same or the opposite. Some few forms of association tests are arranged in this form.

Symonds, P., Measurement in Secondary Education, p. 436.

Sampling. In research it is very commonly desired to study a group so large that all members of the group cannot be included. It therefore becomes necessary to resort to sampling; that is, to the selection of a portion or sample of the whole groups with which it is desired to deal. This sample is then studied and the results obtained considered as applying to the whole group. The sample selected should be so chosen that no bias enters into its selection and should be large enough to yield fairly reliable results. How reliable these results are can ordinarily be determined by measuring errors of sampling. Sampling may be made by selecting every fourth or tenth or other selected case in a random set of scores.

Odell, C. W., Statistical Method in Education, p. 338.

Scale. The word scale is used in two somewhat different yet related senses. In the most restricted of these it designates that portion of a measuring instrument which is used in describing a pupil's performance as contrasted with that portion which secures the pupil's performance. In the case of some of our measuring instruments, such as composition and handwriting scales, the scale itself is the conspicuous feature and the procedure which must be followed in order to secure pupil performances is not a part of the scale. In the case of other measuring instruments, such as common standardized tests in arithmetic and spelling, the scale is less obvious, the test portion of the instrument being prominent. There must be in the case of every measuring instrument, however, some scale composed of units in terms of which pupils' performances are described. In its second sense the word scale is used as synonymous with scaled test.

> Greene, H. A., and Jorgensen, A. N., Use and Interpretation of High School Tests, p. 26.
> Monroe, W. S., Introduction to the Theory of Educational Measurement, pp. 15f., 20f., 106.
> Odell, C. W., Educational Measurement in the High School, pp. 24, 35.
> Orleans, J. S., Measurement in Education, pp. 107, 122.

Scaled Test. A scaled test is a test in which the questions are arranged in order of increasing difficulty. Usually, but not always, the increase in difficulty from one exercise to the next is approximately constant throughout the scale.

> Odell, C. W., Educational Measurement in the High School, pp. 25, 77.
> Orleans, J. S., Measurement in Education, p. 122.
> Symonds, P., Measurement in Secondary Education, pp. 300–302.
> Monroe, W. S., Introduction to the Theory of Educational Measurement, pp. 62, 73f., 78f., 89f., 118f.

Scatter Diagram. Synonymous with correlation graph.

School Survey. A study or investigation of a city, state, or other school system, or in some cases of a single school, which attempts to evaluate the general efficiency thereof and to point out needed changes and improvements. Such a study ordinarily deals with the building program, finances, qualifications and salaries of teachers, pupil achievement, general administration and organization, methods of supervision and teaching, the curriculum, and various other factors. Sometimes a survey is limited in scope.

> Odell, C. W., Educational Measurement in the High School, p. 36.

Scientific. In educational research an investigator may be called scientific when he knows his data and uses them with a complete recognition of any imperfections that may exist either in them or in his procedures. Investigations based on facts are scientific.

Score. A pupil's score is a description of his performance. As distinguished from a mark it is a description in terms of the scale of units used in connection with the given measuring instrument and not in terms of the marking system employed in the school.

> Freeman, F. N., Mental Tests, p. 263.
> Monroe, W. S., DeVoss, J. C. and Kelly, F. J., Educational Tests and Measurements, p. 417f.
> Odell, C. W., Educational Measurement in the High School, p. 442.
> Pressey, S. L., and Cole, L., Introduction to the Use of Standard Tests, pp. 112–118.

Second Quartile (Q_2). Synonymous with median, therefore the expression is rarely used.

Selection of Exercises. In the construction of tests it is usual to secure a large number of exercises first and then to select from this number those to be used in the final test. Such a selection may be in accord with any one or any combination of three criteria or methods, or it may be without the use of any definite criteria. These three criteria are statistical selection, agreement with educational objectives, and suitableness for testing purposes as determined by trial. If no definite criterion is used the selection is said to be arbitrary.

> Monroe, W. S., Introduction to the Theory of Educational Measurements, p. 89f.
> Ruch, G. M., and Stoddard, G. D., Tests and Measurements in High School Instruction, p. 204f.
> Symonds, P., Measurement in Secondary Education, p. 279f.

Selection Test. Sometimes applied to any one of several varieties of objective tests. Among these are the matching test, the test which calls for a rearrangement of items in the correct order, certain varieties of multiple-answer tests, and so forth, where the testee is required to select the correct answer from several suggested answers.

Self-Administering Test. A test in which the directions are given in the test itself. The directions are so definite and clear that the tester needs only to keep order and time the test.

Self-Correlation. This refers to correlation employed for the purpose of measuring reliability of a test. *See correlation, reliable.*

Semi-Interquartile Range. Synonymous with quartile deviation.

Short-Answer Test. Synonymous with new examination.

$\sum$ **(pronounced** Sigma). Usually read, "sum of ——".

σ sigma deviation.

Sigma ($\sum$). The capital sigma is used as the symbol of summation; that is, it indicates that various values of the variable referred to are to be summed or added. For example, the expression $\sum X$ means that all values of the variable X are to be summed.

Sigma (σ). This is the most common abbreviation for the standard deviation or standard error. A subscript is frequently employed with the abbreviation for the standard deviation to indicate the measure to which it belongs or the situation to which it applies. Thus, σ_M denotes the standard deviation or error of the mean; σ_b that of the coefficient of regression; $_{est.}$, the standard error of estimate, and so forth. *See standard deviation.*

Significance. In a technical statistical sense a measure or difference is said to be significant when by comparison with its standard or probable error or some other measure of reliability it is apparent that it is fairly reliable. The most common meaning of significance has to do with sampling; that is, with whether or not the errors resulting from using only a sample are so great as to destroy the significance of the derived measures or conclusions. If a measure or difference is two times its standard error or three times its probable error, it is ordinarily considered significant, though sometimes this ratio is raised to three times the standard error and four or five times the probable error.

Odell, C. W., Statistical Method in Education, p. 350.

Similarities Test. This is a variety of the multiple-answer or association test in which the one or more of several given terms most like one or more other given terms is to be indicated.

Single-Answer Test. A variety of the new examination test question which consists of questions so phrased that the answer to each is a single word. It is ordinarily understood also that the questions are such that there is only one possible correct answer. Some forms of the completion tests illustrate this.

    Odell, C. W., Educational Measurement in the High School, p. 485.
    Ruch, G. M., and Stoddard, G. D., Tests and Measurements in High School Instruction, pp. 267, 272.

Sk. Abbreviation for skewness.

Skew (or Skewed) Distribution. A skew distribution or frequency curve may be thought of as a normal distribution or curve which has been pushed or pulled out in one direction so that one extreme is further from the central tendency than the other. If it has been stretched out so that the end of the distribution at which the largest measures are located is further from the central tendency, the skewness is said to be positive or plus. If the lower end is further from the central tendency, it is said to be negative or minus. The most common formulae for measuring skewness are

$$sk. = \frac{3(M. - Md.)}{\sigma} \text{ and } sk. = \frac{Q_3 + Q_1 - 2Md.}{Q}.$$

    Odell, C. W., Statistical Method in Education, p. 62.
    Otis, A. S., Statistical Method in Educational Measurements, p. 75.

Skewness (Sk.). *See skew distribution.*

Smoothed Curve. In cases in which the data are too few to be truly representative and therefore show irregularities not typical of the whole group being studied, they are smoothed—that is, rounded off—to approximate the distribution that would supposedly be obtained if the sample were adequate in size. The most common method of smoothing consists in substituting for each frequency a new frequency which is the average of the original one and a given number of adjacent frequencies half of which lie on each side of it. The usual number of such adjacent frequencies taken is two, one on each side of the original frequency.

    Odell, C. W., Statistical Method in Education, p. 43.

Social Age. In the same manner as general intelligence is frequently stated in terms of mental age and achievement in terms of achievement or subject age, so social development or maturity is sometimes stated in terms of social age. A social age of a given amount such, for example, as ten years and three months, means that the individual so rated has the maturity that is typical or average for children ten years and three months old.

Social Intelligence. Ability an individual shows in dealing with new situations which involve the relations of persons in a group.
> Pintner, R., Intelligence Testing, p. 55.

Spearman Footrule. A formula devised by C. S. Spearman for computing the coefficient of correlation by the equation

$$R = 1 - \frac{6 \sum g}{N^2 - 1}.$$

> Otis, A. S., Statistical Method in Educational Measurements, pp. 210, 295.

Special Ability Tests. Tests which are designed to measure some special ability or restricted group of capacities.

Speed Test. Synonymous with rate test.

Spiral Test. A spiral test is a cycle test so arranged that there is an increase in difficulty in successive sub-tests or exercises. Most spiral tests are not entirely regular or uniform in increase in difficulty. *See cycle test.*
> Monroe, W. S., Introduction to the Theory of Educational Measurement, pp. 63, 74f.
> Odell, C. W., Educational Measurement in the High School, p. 26.

Split-Half Procedure. Correlation of scores obtained from one half of a test with scores on the other half of the test, a procedure used often to determine the reliability of a test.

Standard. A standard is a statement of the goal or objective which pupils should reach in their performance at a certain time. It is usually stated as an age or grade standard. Standards may be based upon norms but differ from them in that they represent goals of attainment rather than average actual attainment.
> Greene, H. A., and Jorgensen, A. N., Use and Interpretation of High School Tests, pp. 214, 215.
> Ruch, G. M., and Stoddard, G. D., Tests and Measurements in High School Instruction, pp. 16–18.
> Symonds, P., Measurement in Secondary Education, p. 260f.

Standard Deviation (σ or S. D.). The standard deviation is one of the two or three most common measures of deviation or variability used. It is based upon the squares of the actual deviations and is always found about the mean. In a normal distribution or curve it represents the distance from the mean to the point of inflection; that is, the point at which the slope of the curve changes from an angle of more than 45° with the base line to one of less than that amount. Furthermore, in a normal distribution a distance of one standard deviation on each side of the mean includes 34.13 per cent of the area of the curve or, in other words, of the number of cases. Therefore, 68.27 per cent of the cases in a normal distribution lie not more than one standard deviation from the mean. The simple formula for the standard deviation is

$$\sigma = \sqrt{\frac{\sum x^2}{N}}.$$

    Kelley, T. L., Interpretation of Educational Measurements, p. 154f.
    Odell, C. W., Educational Measurement in the High School, pp. 574, 598.
    Odell, C. W., Statistical Method in Education, pp. 57, 98, 123, 132, 137, 439.
    Otis, A. S., Statistical Method in Educational Measurements, pp. 88, 91, 93.

Standard Error (σ). This is merely the standard deviation when used as a measure of errors.

    Odell, C. W., Educational Measurement in the High School, pp. 62, 592, 598.
    Odell, C. W., Statistical Method in Education, p. 326.

Standard Error of Estimate ($\sigma_{est.}$). Refers to the standard error when used as a measure of errors of estimate.

$$\sigma_{est.} = \sigma \sqrt{1 - r^2}.$$

    Monroe, W. S., Introduction to the Theory of Educational Measurement, p. 348f.
    Odell, C. W., Statistical Method in Education, p. 363.

Standard Error of Measurement ($\sigma_{meas.}$). This is merely the standard error used to measure errors of measurement. It is derived from the standard error of estimate.

$$\sigma_{meas.} = \sigma \sqrt{1 - r}.$$

    Monroe, W. S., Introduction to the Theory of Educational Measurement, p. 207f.
    Odell, C. W., Educational Measurement in the High School, pp. 62, 65, 592.
    Odell, C. W., Statistical Method in Education, p. 366.

Standard Score. A means of obtaining scores which can be compared when the original units of measurement are incomparable. Raw scores are converted by using the standard deviation of each set of scores as a unit of measurement and the mean as the zero point. Subtract the mean of the series algebraically from the raw score and divide by the standard deviation of the distribution.

> Odell, C. W., Statistical Method in Education, p. 406.

Standard Test. Synonymous with standardized test in the broader sense.

Standard Unit. A standard unit is one which is understood in the same way, by all persons competent to make use of it. A unit may be made standard by use, by authority, or otherwise.

> Monroe, W. S., Introduction to the Theory of Educational Measurement, p. 17.
> Odell, C. W., Educational Measurement in the High School, p. 12.

Standardized Test. A test is standardized when norms based upon a sufficient number of individuals have been determined for it. Usually a standardized test is understood to have a somewhat broader meaning and to refer to a test which not only has satisfactory norms, but also has been devised scientifically so that it yields relatively objective scores, and has such directions for administration as to secure practical uniformity.

> Greene, H. A., and Jorgensen, A. N., Use and Interpretation of High School Tests, pp. 20, 574, 575.
> Monroe, W. S., DeVoss, J. C., and Kelly, F. J., Educational Tests and Measurements, p. 12.
> Odell, C. W., Educational Measurement in the High School, pp. 12, 21, 471.
> Orleans, J. S., Measurement in Education, p. 42.

Stanford-Binet or Stanford Revision of the Binet Scale. The 1916 or 1936 Revision of the Binet-Simon Scale, an individual test of intelligence. The Terman-Merrill (1936) is the most recent revision.

> Freeman, F. N., Mental Tests, pp. 90–96.
> Odell, C. W., Educational Measurement in the High School, pp. 33, 144, 395, 400, 403.
> Pintner, R., Intelligence Testing, pp. 149–156.

Statistical Method (or Methods). Any method of research or investigation which involves mathematical operations used in the interpretation of data.

Statistical Selection of Exercises. A method of selecting the exercises to be included in a test from the large number usually collected is known as the method of statistical selection. According to this the per cent of correct responses for each exercise is determined and from these data the difficulty of each computed. The exercises then selected are those whose degrees of difficulty are appropriate. The selection may be items of the same difficulty or items of increasing difficulty.

Statistics. The science and art which gathers and coordinates numerous facts and treats these facts mathematically so that the relation between them may be shown clearly and the conclusions free from anomalies due to the chance factor.

Subject. This term has two meanings in the field of testing: 1. the self or experiencing individual. 2. any topic or area of knowledge.

Subject Age (S. A.). Synonymous with achievement age, except that subject age is used only in connection with single subjects, never with an average age in several subjects. *See achievement age, educational age.*

    Odell, C. W., Educational Measurement in the High School, p. 444.

Subject-Matter Test. Synonymous with achievement test.

Subject Quotient (S. Q.). The subject quotient is found in the same general manner as an achievement quotient; that is, by dividing a pupil's score expressed in terms of subject age by his chronological age. Thus

$$S.\ Q. = \frac{S.\ A.}{C.\ A.}.$$

The expression is used only in connection with separate subjects. *See achievement quotient, educational quotient.*

Subject Ratio (S. R.). This expression is very rarely used. It refers to the quotient obtained by dividing a pupil's score in a particular subject expressed in terms of subject age by his mental age. It is, therefore, synonymous with the achievement quotient in the ordinary sense of the latter. *See achievement quotient.*

Subjective. A measuring instrument is said to be subjective when different results are secured by different persons, or by the same person at different times, using it to measure the same thing. Various factors may cause subjectivity, such as method of giving tests, scoring tests, or interpreting test results.

    Monroe, W. S., Introduction to the Theory of Educational Measurement, p. 26f.

Subjective Trait. A trait which is not easily measured in terms of any standard performance.

Subjectivity. *See subjective.*

Sub-Normal. Below normal, less than normal.

Sub-Test. A sub-test is one of the major divisions of a test or measuring instrument. All the exercises within each sub-test are of the same general form or type. Many tests are not divided into subjects and hence may be thought of as consisting of just one sub-test.

Survey. Synonymous with school survey.

Survey Test. Synonymous with general survey test.

Syllable-Span Test. Similar to a digit-span test except that syllables are used instead of digits.

Symbol-Digit Test. A substitution test.

Systematic Error. An error due to the manner of collecting data, to be contrasted with incidental error.
> Odell, C. W., Statistical Method in Education, p. 336.

T

Table of Double Entry. Synonymous with correlation table.

10–90 Percentile (D). The distance between the tenth and the ninetieth percentiles has been suggested and used as a measure of deviation or variability. In formula form, $D = P_{90} - P_{10}$.
> Odell, C. W., Statistical Method in Education, pp. 118–119.

Test. Used in a general sense to designate any type of instrument for measuring mental capacity or ability of any sort. In this usage it includes instruments which have been designated tests by their authors and likewise those which have been called scales, as well as ordinary examinations. It is sometimes used to designate parts or even specific age level units used in the Stanford-Binet, such as the Ball-and-Field Test.
> Greene, H. A. and Jorgensen, A. N., Use and Interpretation of High School Tests, p. 10.
> Odell, C. W., Educational Measurement in the High School, pp. 24, 35.
> Orleans, J. S., Measurement in Education, p. 65.

Tetrachoric r. The coefficient of correlation between two variables each of which can have only two values. For example, tetrachoric r might be used to express the relationship between sex and success or failure in a given course.

    Odell, C. W., Statistical Method in Education, p. 311.

Tetrad Difference Criterion. Where 1, 2, 3, and 4 represent four tests or variables and r is the product-moment coefficient of correlation, $r_{12} \, r_{34}$ is a tetrad difference. Spearman states that if this and other tetrad differences are zero the several correlations may be thought of as due to a factor which is common to all tests and four factors or groups of factors, each specific to tests 1, 2, 3, and 4 respectively. This has also been known as the factor theory of mental organization.

    Pintner, R., Intelligence Testing, pp. 62–68.

Third Quartile (Q_3). The third quartile is that point on the scale of measurement used in connection with any distribution at or below which three-fourths and at or above which one-fourth of the measures fall. Its formula is

$$Q_3 = 1 + \frac{\frac{3N}{4} - S}{f}.$$

See quartile.

    Odell, C. W., Educational Measurement in the High School, pp. 562, 598.
    Odell, C. W., Statistical Method in Education, p. 105.

Time-Limit Procedure. A procedure used when pupils are allowed to work on tests only a certain length of time. The accomplishment or score of the pupil is determined by the amount done during this time. This is in contrast to the non-timed test.

Timed Test. A timed test is for practical purposes synonymous with a rate test.

Trade Test. A test designed to measure a person's actual ability in a trade or a vocation. A sample of the actual trade processes is generally used.

    Greene, H. A., and Jorgensen, A. N., Use and Interpretation of High School Tests, pp. 537–540.

Traditional Examination. This term has come to be frequently applied to examinations of the essay type commonly used. Such examinations consist of exercises which require pupils to discuss, summarize, outline, criticise, compare, reorganize, evaluate, state, show, analyze, and so forth. The term is used in contrast to new examination and is, therefore, generally understood to include tests or examinations which are relatively subjective and require a considerable amount of writing on the part of pupils.

> Odell, C. W., Educational Measurement in the High School, pp. 13, 473, 482.
> Orleans, J. S., Measurement in Education, p. 37.
> Ruch, G. M., and Stoddard, G. D., Tests and Measurements in High School Instruction, p. 252f.
> Symonds, P., Measurement in Secondary Education, pp. 3-5, 417, 418, 431, 441, 472.

Transmuted Score. A transmuted score is one which has been changed from its original form or numerical value as a point score yielded directly by a test into an equivalent score on some other basis or manner of interpretation. *See derived score, transmutation of scores.*

> Odell, C. W., Educational Measurement in the High School, p. 80, 442.
> Otis, A. S., Statistical Method in Educational Measurements, p. 119.

Transmutation of Scores. The transmutation or changing of scores generally refers to the changing of point scores—that is, scores yielded directly by a test or scale—into ratings of some other sort, such as age scores, T-scores, school marks, and so forth. Sometimes also point scores on one or more tests are transmuted so as to be equivalent to scores on another test or perhaps all are changed to some common basis for purposes of comparing, combining, averaging, or other computation, such as the method used in the New Stanford Achievement Test.

> Monroe, W. S., Introduction to the Theory of Educational Measurement, p. 211f.
> Otis, A. S., Statistical Method in Educational Measurements, p. 119f.

True-False Test. An alternative test which consists of a number of statements the truth or falsity of which is to be indicated by those being tested, is called a true-false test. This form of exercise is rather commonly used in connection with new-type examinations and standardized tests.

> Greene, H. A., and Jorgensen, A. N., Use and Interpretation of High School Tests, p. 83.
> McCall, W. A., How to Measure in Education, pp. 119-134.

Monroe, W. S., Introduction to the Theory of Educational Measurement, p. 283.
Odell, C. W., Educational Measurements in the High School, p. 489.
Ruch, G. M., and Stoddard, G. D., Tests and Measurements in High School Instruction, pp. 268, 275.

True Score. A pupil's true score may be defined as the average of an infinite number of measurements of the characteristic being measured. These measurements should be made under the same conditions. It is, of course, impossible to fulfill either the ideal of an infinite number of measurements or that of the same conditions. Even though other conditions are controlled as well as possible, practice effect enters in and in general causes higher scores to be made on the second trial of the test than on the first, and so on. Therefore, in some cases an approximation to a true score is obtained which consists of the average of a fairly large number of measurements corrected as well as possible for practice effect and other differences in the testing conditions. The concept of a true score is frequently helpful even though such a score cannot actually be found and certain statistical calculations concerning true scores can be made even though the scores themselves cannot be determined.

Monroe, W. S., Introduction to the Theory of Educational Measurement, p. 201f.
Odell, C. W., Statistical Method in Education, pp. 248, 366.
Ruch, G. M., and Stoddard, G. D., Tests and Measurements in High School Instruction, pp. 369-372.

T-Scale. The T-scale, so named in honor of Terman and Thorndike, is a scale based upon the distribution of ability of an average or complete group of twelve-year-old pupils. It consists of 100 units of .1 standard deviation each and extends from five standard deviations below the mean of twelve-year-old pupil ability to five standard deviations above the mean. For pupils whose abilities are not too different from those of twelve-year-pupils it provides a basis for derived scores which may be compared with one another though derived from different tests. A rather large number of standardized tests provide tables by which point scores may be transmuted into T-scores.

McCall, W. A., How to Measure in Education, p. 272f.
Monroe, W. S., Introduction to the Theory of Educational Measurements, p. 150f.
Odell, C. W., Educational Measurements in the High School, p. 447.

T-Score. A score given according to the T-scale.
>Greene, H. A., and Jorgensen, A. N., Use and Interpretation of High School Tests, pp. 185–186.
>McCall, W. A., How to Measure in Education, pp. 72–75, 142, 272–307.
>Monroe, W. S., Introduction to the Theory of Educational Measurements, p. 201.
>Odell, C. W., Statistical Method in Education, pp. 391, 407.
>Otis, A. S., Statistical Method in Educational Measurements, p. 122.
>Symonds, P., Measurement in Secondary Education, p. 385.

Two-Factor Theory. A theory advanced by Spearman that all modes of cognitive activity have in common one fundamental factor or group of factors (g) and specific elements (s) differing in the same individual for different abilities.
>Freeman, F. N., Mental Tests, p. 68.
>Pintner, R., Intelligence Testing, pp. 62–68.

Two-Groups Method. This is synonymous with the equivalent groups method when only two groups of pupils are employed.

U

Undistributed Scores. In the cases of some of our measuring instruments the easiest exercises are so difficult that pupils who make scores of zero may represent a considerable range in ability. In the case of others the most difficult exercises are so easy or the time so long, or both, that a number of pupils frequently make perfect scores and thus no complete information is secured as to the extent of their abilities. Furthermore, in some tests the scale units employed are so large or the difference in difficulty between successive exercises so great that there may be considerable differences in the abilities of pupils who earn the same score. In such cases as these it is said that the scores of the pupils whose abilities differ but who receive the same scores in so far as a given test is concerned are undistributed. *See discrimination.*
>McCall, W. A., How to Measure in Education, pp. 240, 250, 251.
>Symonds, P., Measurement in Secondary Education, p. 301.

Uniform Test. Synonymous with rate test.

Unimodal. A frequency distribution having but a single mode is said to be unimodal.
>Odell, C. W., Statistical Method in Education, p. 90.

Unreliability. *See reliability.*

Unreliable. *See reliable.*

Upper Quartile (Q_3). Synonymous with third quartile.

V

Valid. A measuring instrument is commonly said to be valid if it fulfills the function which it is intended or stated to perform. It may lack validity either because it is unreliable, due to subjective administration and scoring, or because it measures some other ability or abilities than its function specifies. Thus a test cannot be valid unless it is objective and reliable, but can be perfectly objective and reliable without being valid. Since few, if any, tests possess perfect validity, the term is used in a relative sense, and the tests are said to be valid when they approximate validity. It has also been suggested that the term valid should be used in a more restricted sense. In this sense it would exclude the factor of reliability. That is to say, a measuring instrument would be called valid if it performed its stated function better than any other which might be stated for it regardless of how well it did so. Thus a test might be so unreliable that little confidence could be placed in the scores obtained from it, but if they were better measures of its stated function than of anything else it would be valid.

> Brueckner, L. J., and Melby, E. O., Diagnostic and Remedial Teaching, p. 80.
> Kelley, T. L., Interpretation of Educational Measurements, pp. 13–14, 29–31.
> Monroe, W. S., Introduction to the Theory of Educational Measurements, p. 188f.
> Odell, C. W., Educational Measurements in the High School, pp. 11, 52.
> Pintner, R., Intelligence Testing, pp. 104–112.
> Symonds, P., Measurement in Secondary Education, pp. 279–286.

Validation. *See valid.*

Validity. *See valid.*

Variable. A characteristic or trait which may exist in different amounts. It is also used in the following sense, in that the quality of pupils' handwriting differs, since that of one pupil may possess a certain degree of merit, that of another pupil a different degree, and so forth; therefore quality of handwriting also is a variable. Because almost all of the traits dealt with in educational research are variable, the term is very commonly used to refer to the two or more traits or characteristics which are compared, correlated, or dealt with in some other way.

>McCall, W. A., How to Measure in Education, pp. 30-32.
>Odell, C. W., Statistical Method in Education, pp. 14, 33.

Variable Error. Variable errors differ for the different members of a group as contrasted with constant errors which tend to be the same for a whole group. Approximately half of the variable errors in a given group are positive and the other half negative, usually, however, a few being zero. The distinguishing characteristics of variable errors are that they differ from pupil to pupil and that ordinarily the magnitude of the variable error in the case of any given individual cannot be determined. It is, however, practically always possible to make statements as to the general size and distribution of the variable errors in a group and as to the chances that the variable error does or does not exceed a certain magnitude in the case of any particular individual. From the standpoint of effect upon derived measures, variable errors differ from constant errors in that they do not affect measures of central tendency—that is, averages—but do tend to lower coefficients of correlations. Just the reverse is true of constant errors. *See constant error.*

>Monroe, W. S., Introduction to the Theory of Educational Measurements, pp. 198f., 243, 329f., 344.
>Odell, C. W., Educational Measurement in the High School, p. 69.
>Odell, C. W., Statistical Method in Education, p. 56, 336.
>Symonds, P., Measurement in Secondary Education, p. 352.

Variability. Synonymous with deviation.

Verbal Test. Sometimes all tests in which either the examiner or the subjects make use of spoken or written language are called verbal. On other occasions the term is applied only to those tests in which the subjects must respond by written or spoken language and not to those in which oral directions are given by the examiner with no verbal responses by the subjects.

>Freeman, F. N., Mental Tests, p. 257f.
>Odell, C. W., Educational Measurement in the High School, p. 27.

Vocabulary Test. A random sample of the words in a complete general dictionary. These are presented to the testee for definition and his score is an index of his total vocabulary.

>Greene, H. A., and Jorgensen, A. N., Use and Interpretation of High School Tests, p. 362.

Odell, C. W., Educational Measurement in the High School, p. 132.
Symonds, P., Measurement in Secondary Education, pp. 106–109.

Vocational Guidance. This refers to the directing or advising of individuals with regard to choosing their vocations or occupations. No hard and fast line can be drawn between it and educational guidance as much of one is frequently necessary in connection with the other.

Jones, A. J., Principles of Guidance, pp. 281, 304, 316, 361.
McCall, W. A., How to Measure in Education, p. 169f.
Monroe, W. S., DeVoss, J. C., and Kelly, F. J., Educational Tests and Measurements, p. 456.
Odell, C. W., Educational Measurement in the High School, p. 520.
Symonds, P., Measurement in Secondary Education, p. 19.

W

Weighting. The determination of the proportional part to be played by each of a number of items or factors in determining a total or average score or measure is called weighting. The most frequent need for determining weights is in connection with the various exercises or other parts of a test or examination. If a correct response to one exercise is given a credit of three points, that to another of two, and to a third of one, the weights of these exercises are said to be respectively three, two, and one. A test in which all exercises count the same number of points, frequently one for each, is sometimes said to be unweighted, but improperly so, since the exercises are in reality equally weighted. In the cases of many standardized tests weights have been assigned in accordance with rather careful determinations of difficulty. In other standardized tests the determining factor has been the relative or supposed relative importance of the exercises. Other plans of weighting, some of which are merely modifications of the two described, have also been used. Experimental studies have shown that unless the number of items is small or the differences in weights very great, the relative scores of pupils will differ little, if all exercises or items are weighted equally, from what they will be if weights are carefully determined. In a similar fashion to that just described, weighting is also necessary in determining pupils' standings for the semester or year from their marks upon oral recitation, short quizzes, outside written work, notebooks, laboratory work, final examinations, and any other elements considered. Weighting also frequently enters into the determination of a criterion measure, in which case a number of different measures are frequently combined into one.

    Freeman, F. N., Mental Tests, p. 272f.
    Monroe, W. S., Introduction to the Theory of Educational Measurements, p. 116f.
    Otis, A. S., Statistical Method in Educational Measurements, pp. 120, 131, 240.

X, Y, Z

X, x. In dealing with situations in which two variables are concerned, such as a correlation table, the coefficient and ratio of correlation, the regression equations, and so forth, it is very common to refer to one of them by the term X. If they are in a correlation table the one so referred to is that which has its scale upon the horizontal axis. Whenever X is used to refer to the variable itself, x is used to refer to the difference or deviation of the variable from its mean. *See correlation table, variable.*

    Odell, C. W., Statistical Method in Education, pp. 37f., 151f.

Y, y. In dealing with situations in which two variables are concerned, such as a correlation table, the coefficient and ratio of correlation, the regression equations, and so forth, it is very common to refer to one of them by the term Y. If they are in a correlation table the one so referred to is that which has its scale upon the vertical axis. Whenever Y is used to refer to the variable itself, y is used to refer to the difference or deviation of the variable from its mean. *See correlation table, variable.*

    Odell, C. W., Statistical Method in Education, pp. 37f., 151f.

Yes-No Test. This is a variety of the alternative test commonly used in connection with the new examination and with standardized tests. It consists of a series of questions to each one of which pupils are expected to respond by yes or no.

    Odell, C. W., Educational Measurement in the High School, p. 489.
    Greene, H. A., and Jorgensen, A. N., Use and Interpretation of High School Tests, p. 84.
    Symonds, P., Measurement in Secondary Education, p. 31.

Z. Abbreviation for mode.

Zero Point. The zero point on any given scale is the point which means just not any of the trait or characteristic measured by that scale. In the case of most educational measuring instruments a score of zero does not represent zero ability, or, in other words, a pupil who earns a score of zero cannot be known to be located at the true zero point. This result follows from the fact that the easiest exercises on most tests are difficult enough that a pupil may have some knowledge or ability along the line tested and still not be able to respond correctly to the easiest exercise on the test. If scores on different tests are expressed in terms of a common unit they can, for some purposes at least, be added to and subtracted from one another without the determination of true zero points, but they cannot be multiplied and divided into one another unless such points have been found.

McCall, W. A., How to Measure in Education, pp. 291–296.
Monroe, W. S., Introduction to the Theory of Educational Measurements, pp. 101f., 146f., 150.
Odell, C. W., Educational Measurement in the High School, p. 453.
Odell, C. W., Statistical Method in Education, pp. 141, 374.
Symonds, P., Measurement in Secondary Education, p. 301.